Python

Data

Visualization

***

An Easy Introduction to Data Visualization in Python with Matplotlip, Pandas, and Seaborn

*

Step-by-Step Tutorial for Beginners

Samuel Burns

Python Data Visualization: An Easy Introduction to Data Visualization in Python

Editor: Maria Rica/GlobaltechNTC

Editorial Assistant: Zokolodni Sergey

E-Media Editor: Daniel Soler

Book Design: Rebecca.

Collection : **(Step-by-Step Guide For Beginners)**

Publisher: **Amazon KDP Printing and Publishing**

Contact: **globaltechntc@bk.ru**

ISBN: 9781701860254

Imprint: Independently published

First Edition: october 2019

CONTENTS

INTRODUCTION 4

1-BASICS OF DATA VISUALIZATION 6

What is Data Visualization? 6
Why Visualize Data? 7
Data Visualization Techniques 8
Diagrams and Matrices 10

2-BASIC AND SPECIALIZED DATA VISUALIZATION
TOOLS 11

Basic Data Visualization Tools 11
Specialized Data Visualization Tools 14
IBM Watson Analytics 15

3-ADVANCED VISUALIZATIONS TOOLS 18

Openheatmap 18
Leaflet 19
Chartbuilder 19
Open Refine 20
Google Data Studio 20

4-EXPLORING THE LIBRARIES 22

Matplotlib 22
Pandas 23
Seaborn 25
Folium 26

5-DATA VISUALIZATION WITH MATPLOTLIB 27

Chart Properties 27
Chart Styling 32

6-DATA VISUALIZATION WITH PANDAS 58

7-DATA VISUALIZATION WITH SEABORN 90

Distributional Plots *91*

Categorical Plots *101*

Combined Violin and Swarm Plots *122*

8-CREATING MAPS AND VISUALIZING GEOSPATIAL
DATA..161

The Dataset *161*

Exploration...*162*

Creating the Interactive Map...*169*

CONCLUSION 173

ABOUT THE AUTHOR 176

Introduction

Today, a lot of data is available for processing. This data is generated by blogs, social websites and web pages. This data carries a lot of information. However, there is a need for a way that will help businesses transform the data into information. Natural Language Processing is one of such tools. It is a branch of artificial intelligence that deals with machines understanding natural languages such as English. It is through natural language processing that computers can understand human speech.

Companies usually generate data in huge volumes, running up to gigabytes. It may be hard for companies to process such data manually. However, with natural language processing, a computer can be trained to process text written in a natural language and extract information from it. This means that the computer will be able to identify the nouns, verbs, adjectives, punctuation marks, etc. contained in the text. Through natural language processing, we can identify the attitude of the person who wrote a particular text. The computer will able to tell how positive or negative a certain text is. Due to this, businesses have benefited a lot from natural language processing as they can analyze customer feedback on their products to know how positive or negative they are towards their products.

This book is an excellent guide for you to learn natural language processing in detail. The author guides you on how to perform natural language processing tasks in Python programming language. You will also learn how to set up and use the Natural Language Processing Toolkit (NLTK).

1-Basics of Data Visualization

What is Data Visualization?

Data visualization refers to the graphical representation of data and information. By use of visual elements such as graphs, charts, and maps, data visualization tools provide us with an easy way of identifying and understanding outliers, trends, and patterns in data.

In the Big Data world, data visualization tools and technologies are good for analyzing massive amounts of information and facilitate the making of data-driven decisions.

Trends, patterns, and correlations may be difficult to detect and understand in text-based data. However, by use of data visualization software, these may be easier to detect and understand.

The data visualization tools of today go beyond the generation of standard graphs and charts like those provided in Microsoft Excel Spreadsheets. They can be used for the representation of data in more sophisticated ways such as dials and gauges, infographics, sparklines, geographic maps, heat maps, and detailed fever, bar and pie charts. Some of the images come with interactive capabilities, allowing users to manipulate them or drill into the data for the purposes of querying and analysis. There can also be indicators designed in such a way that they alert the user when an update is done on the data or when a set condition is met.

Why Visualize Data?

Data visualization has become a source of intelligence for modern businesses. The leading vendors in the area of business intelligence, Tableau and Qlik have put much emphasis on data visualization, and this has made other software vendors focus more on data visualization.

Our eyes tend to be drawn more to colors and patterns. It is easy for us to differentiate between a square and a circle, red and blue. We have been used to a visual culture such as art, TV ads, and movies.

Data visualization is a special type of visual art that can easily grab our attention and keep the eyes on the message. After seeing a chart, we can quickly identify trends and outliers. The following are some of the advantages associated with data visualization:

1. Improved sight

With data visualization, you can get insights that you cannot get from the traditional descriptive statistics. If you have different datasets, it is easy for you to see their different trends by use of data visualization. This means that it is always good for us to visualize data instead of relying on descriptive statistics only.

2.   Faster decision making

Every business is facing stiff competition in the marketplace. A business that is able to gather data quickly and act on it before the competition will be more competitive. Speed is of essence, and with data visualization, we can be able to analyze large quantities of data within a short period of time.

3.   Discover emerging trends

Data visualization is a great tool to help you discover trends in both the business and the market. You can easily detect outliers that affect the quality of your product. After the identification, you can take the appropriate action before the problem becomes bigger.

4.   Communicate the outcome to others

Once you have identified the trends underlying your data, it will be easy for you to communicate the insights to the others. In this step, you have to look for the best way to represent your data visually so that they may find it easy to understand.

Data Visualization Techniques

Visualization marks the first step in getting to understand data. There are a variety of techniques that a data analyst can use to present data and show the correlations. Before visualizing data, you have to choose the right method to use. There is a visualization technique that is most suitable for the type of data that you have. This means that choosing the right visualization technique is key to ensuring that the data is understood.

Here are the common data visualization techniques that you can choose for your data:

Charts

This provides the easiest way of showing the development of either one or more data sets. There are different types of charts that you can use to visualize your data. Examples include bar and line charts that can be used for showing the relationships between elements over time and pie charts that show the proportions of the elements of one whole.

Plots

With plots, you can distribute two or more data sets over a 2D or 3D space so as to show the relationships between the sets as well as their parameters on the plot. Plots are also of different types, with bubble and scatter plots being the traditional ones. For the cases of big data, data analysts normally use box plots since they can show relationships large volumes of various data.

Maps

Maps are widely used in different types of industries. They allow the positioning of elements on relevant areas and objects-building plans, geographical maps, website layouts, etc. Some of the common maps are heat maps, cartograms, and dot distribution maps.

Diagrams and Matrices

Diagrams are used for showing complex relationships between data and links and different types of data can be included in a single visualization. Diagrams can be tree-like, multidimensional or hierarchical.

A matrix is a technique for data visualization technique that helps in reflecting the correlations between multiple data sets that are updated constantly like in streaming.

2-Basic and Specialized Data Visualization Tools

There are many different software tools that have been developed for data visualization. New visualization solutions are also being discovered every day. Some are available for free while others are available for purchase. The different visualization tools are designed and developed for different levels of specialization. Some are for creating basic visualizations while others are good for creating complex visualizations.

Let us discuss these tools:

Basic Data Visualization

Tools

Tableau

Tableau is one of the data visualization tools available in the market. Its users are provided with Drag and Drop functionality, help them to easily design charts, maps, matrix reports, tabular, dashboards and stories without any technical skills.

With Tableau, one can establish a connection to files, Big Data and relational sources to get data and process it. It also allows for real-time collaboration and data blending, which gives it some uniqueness. It is highly used for visual data analysis in academic institutions, businesses, and government organizations.

Before getting started with Tableau, you must first install it into your computer. You should download the Tableau desktop by vising the Products section page of www.tableau.com. The good thing with the tool is that it comes with a free trial version that can be downloaded and installed for free.

FusionCharts

This is a JavaScript library for data visualization. It is one of the best paid for market visualization libraries. You can use this library to create more than 90 different types of charts, and it can be integrated with a wide variety of platforms and frameworks providing you with much flexibility.

There is a great feature that has made FusionCharts the best tool for visualization. Instead of starting to create your chart from scratch, you are provided with a huge number of chart templates that you only need to load your data and have it customized to show the trends and patterns underlying your dataset.

Datawrapper

This tool is becoming a common visualization tool amongst media stations that use charts to present statistics. The tool provides a simple interface, making it easy for one to load their CSV (comma separated values) data and generate straightforward charts. One can also use the tool to create maps that are easy to integrate into reports.

Visme

This is another tool that can help you turn your boring data into more engaging content. It allows you to create engaging presentations, infographics and several other types of engaging content.

The tool provides you with already existing templates that you can use for your data. If you need to create your custom design from scratch, you can rely on content blocks. You will also be provided with millions of icons, images, and fonts.

Highcharts

This one requires a license for you to use it, just like FusionCharts. However, it comes with a trial-version and it can be used for free for personal tasks. You don't need specialized training to be able to use this tool. The success of this can be attributed to its cross-browser support, meaning you can create and

use its visual presentations from different web browsers, which is
not the case with most new platforms.

Specialized Data Visualization Tools

These are the tools that provide a way of creating more
sophisticated visualizations and at the same time, a way of doing
analysis on the data. Let is discuss them:

Sisense

This is another visualization tool that comes with full-stack
analytics capabilities. It is a cloud-based platform that provides
drag and drops capabilities. It can also handle multiple data
sources and it supports natural language queries.

Through its drag and drop feature, it is easy for one to create
charts and other complex graphics and other interactive
visualizations. It can be used for gathering multiple sources of data
into one repository that is easily accessible and which can be
queried instantaneously through dashboards. Such dashboards are
sharable across organizations, ensuring that even the staff with
minimum technical skills can get answers to their queries.

Qlikview

This is the greatest competitor of Tableau. It is used in over
100 countries and its users have liked it for its wide range of
features and highly customizable setup. This also means that it will

take much time for you to become familiar with the tool and use it to its potential.

Other than its great data visualization capabilities, Qlikview provides its users with business intelligence, enterprise reporting, and analytics capabilities and it provides a clutter-free user interface. It is commonly used together with its sister package called Qliksense which is good for data exploration and discovery. It also has strong community support and there are numerous third-party resources that can help its users know how to integrate it with their projects.

IBM Watson Analytics

This is a good tool for data visualization, made unique by its natural language processing capabilities. The platform provides capabilities for conversational data control together with strong data reporting and dashboard building tools. However, this tool is not cheap; hence, it should only be used for serious data analytics and visualization tasks.

Power BI

Power BI is a tool provided by Microsoft for free to provide its users and businesses with a way of analyzing and gaining insights from their data. It is a good tool for non-technical business users to aggregate, visualize, analyze and share their data. It provides an easy to use user interface similar to that offered by Microsoft Excel, and it can be integrated with other Microsoft Office tools, increasing its usefulness. This also makes it a versatile tool that users can start to use without the need for upfront training.

The tool was designed and developed to be used by small and mid-sized business owners. It also comes with a Power BI Plus which can only be used at a monthly subscription fee of less than $10.00 per license. The tool comes in different versions, including a web-based SaaS version (Software as a Service) called Power BI, a Windows 10 application that is downloadable and known as Power Bi Desktop and native mobile apps for Android, Windows and iOS devices.

Power PI comes with a number of tools that help it connect to a wide number of data sources including Microsoft products, Salesforce, and even several other vendors. The developers can easily change how the reporting tools and default visualizations look like, that is appearance, and even import new tools into the platform.

Grafana

This is a data analytics and visualization tool that supports more than 30 sources of data, including Elasticsearch, AWS, and Prometheus.

Note that when it comes to integrations, Grafana is better compared to Kibana, but every system works better with its data type. Grafana is known to be good for the various metrics it provides to its users. Due to this, Grafana has become the best tool amongst the various IoT data visualization tools.

With Grafana, you can visualize and compile into complex

dynamic dashboards the various types of metrics data. It is also good for control and monitoring systems because of its ability to provide different admin roles.

Alerts and notifications can be generated based on a set of predefined rules. It has numerous perks that are good for faster data analytics, like making annotations, creation of custom filters and addition of metadata to various events on the dashboard.

3-Advanced Visualizations Tools

Let us discuss some of the available advanced data visualization tools:

Openheatmap

With this tool, you can transform your spreadsheet, most probably the one with geographical data, into a functional heat map with just a single click. Openheatmap expects you to have your data in a Google Spreadsheet, so your data in an Excel spreadsheet should be transferred into a Google Spreadsheet. This is a trivial process when you compare it to the results that you will get from the tool.

Leaflet

This tool is not good for complete beginners since it is a JavaScript library that you should incorporate into your data visualization framework. However, the good thing with this tool is that it is lightweight, only 33 KB. The tool does not simply create maps, but interactive maps that are good for use on mobile devices. Such a feature is not even available in some of the commercial data visualization tools, showing how powerful Leaflet is. If you like using the command line tool or creating an Application Programming Interface (API), go for the Leaflet library.

Chartbuilder

This is a popular tool for creating charts developed and made available by Quartz, a financial news website, in 2013. Quartz had developed the tool to be used in-house by its journalists to make their news visual. However, the Chartbuilder tool is not much pretty on its own and it's not easy for use by beginners. You are required to know how to download, install the tool and activate a Python script within it.

However, after the setup, you will only have to copy your data and paste it into the tool and then you will be able to generate graphics that you can modify on your style sheets. However, the tool has a downside in that it does not generate more interactive graphics like it is the case with other tools. The tool can only be used for generating static charts that are very polished within only a few steps.

Open Refine

Most people overlook data transformation, a process that is very useful when it comes to data visualization. This even becomes more useful when you are getting your data from different sources such as spreadsheets, logs showing long transactions from machine learning algorithms, etc.

Data transformation is the process of taking a set of disparate numbers and turning them into a set of relatable data. This means that there is cleaning of data, transforming it and making it available to the external tools such as web pages. If you always find these tasks daunting, it will be good for you to use the Open Refine tool. It initially began to exist under Google's flag but it now exists on its own. If you have a bunch of mismatched data at your disposal, then consider using this tool to refine the data.

Google Data Studio

The Google Data Studio is one of the Google Marketing platforms and it allows its users to come up with multiple views of their data and dashboards instead of simply creating one-time and publication-ready visualizations. However, it is a bit difficulty to use and one has to go through a learning curve before they can become an expert in using it. it can be easily integrated with the Google Analytics tool.

Plotly

This tool is more complex compared to Tableau and it comes with analytics perks. You can use this tool to create charts with R and Python, develop custom data analytics apps with Python. It can also be integrated with rich and open source libraries for R, Python, and JavaScript.

Kibana

This is a component of Elastic Stack that helps in turning data into visual insights. It was designed and developed to be used only on Elasticsearch data. However, Kibana is still the best tool for visualization of log data.

With this tool, you can create all types of data visualization techniques, including interactive maps, charts, histograms, and many others. This tool also goes past traditional dashboards for data analytics and visualization.

With Kibana, you can build advanced analytics, combine visualizations from various sources to explore the unique correlations between various insights then use machine learning features to unearth the hidden patterns and relationships between the data events.

4-Exploring the Libraries

In this book, we will be discussing data visualization in Python using three libarries namely:

- Matplotlib
- Pandas
- Seaborn

Matplotlib

This is a Python library used for creating 2D graphs and plots using Python scripts. It has a module called *pyplot* that makes plotting easy by providing features for controlling font properties, line styles, formatting axes, etc. It can be used for creating different types of plots including histograms, power spectra, bar charts, error charts, etc. It is used together with the NumPy library. This means that it is used on the NumPy arrays.

The library was developed in 2002 by John Hunter. The installation of matplotlib can be done using the pip package manager which comes with Python. If you have installed Python on your computer, you already have pip. In Python 3.X, we invoke the package manager using the *pip3* command. The installation can be done by running the following command on the terminal of the operating system:

```
pip3 install matplotlib
```

To verify whether the installation was successful or not, just try to import the *pyplot* module from the library by running the following command from the Python terminal:

```
from matplotlib import pyplot as plt
```

If the installation was successful, you will get back the Python terminal as shown below:

If not, an error will be generated.

Pandas

This is an open source Python package that comes with many tools for data analysis. With Pandas, one is provided with numerous data structures that they can use for storage of their data as well as manipulation of the same data. The library provides numerous methods that can be invoked for data analysis tasks.

Note that the Pandas library was built on Matplotlib. This explains why it comes with features for data visualization. Pandas allow you to create different types of visualizations from your data stored in a dataframe. The good thing with Pandas is that it allows you to load that is stored in various types of formats.

The installation of Pandas can be done using the pip package manager. This package manager comes with Python just as we stated earlier. To install Pandas, run the following command on the terminal of your operating system:

```
pip3 install pandas
```

I have used the *pip3* command since I am using Python 3.X on my system.

To know whether the installation was successful or not, just try to import the Pandas library by running the following command on the Python terminal:

```
import pandas as pd
```

If the installation was successful, you will get back the Python terminal as shown below:

```
>>> import pandas as pd
>>>
```

If the installation was not successful, an error will be generated.

Seaborn

This is a library used for data visualization and it is based on the Matplotlib library. With Seaborn, you can create pretty charts. The library is good at facilitating other data visualization needs such as mapping of color to a variable or the use of faceting. The Seaborn library works well with data stored in a Pandas data frame.

The tool provides its users with a lot of flexibility when creating plots since the user can choose from a wide range of plotting styles. The library is good at mapping the features to your data in an efficient manner.

The installation of the Seaborn library can be done using the pip package manager. Just run the following command on the terminal of your operating system:

```
pip3 install seaborn
```

To verify whether the installation was successful or not, you should import the library by running the following command on the Python terminal:

```
import seaborn as sns
```

If the installation was successful, you should get the Python terminal as shown below:

If the installation was not successful, you will get an error.

Folium

In Python, geographic data is plotted using the *folium* library. Using this library, one can create the map of any place, provide the longitude and the latitude values of the area are known. Also, the folium library generates interactive maps, allowing one to zoom the map in and out after it has been rendered, a very useful feature.

With the folium library, you are able to create various types of leaflet maps. Due to the interactive nature of the maps generated by the folium library, the library has become useful for use in dashboard buildings.

Before using the folium library, we are required to install it. This can be done using the pip package manager. You only have to run the following command from the terminal of your operating system:

```
pip3 install folium
```

The installation will take seconds to minutes before completing it.

5-Data Visualization with Matplotlib

Chart Properties

As we stated earlier, the matplotlib package comes with a module named *pyplot* that helps us in creating plots. For us to use it, we should first import it from the package using the following Python command:

```
import matplotlib.pyplot as plt
```

Any other required libraries can be imported by the use of the necessary commands. To import the dataset to be used for creating the plots, we can use the Pandas library methods such as *read_csv* for reading csv data. The method can be invoked as shown below:
```
pd.read_csv()
```
To create a line plot, use the *plt.plot()* function. There are also other plotting functions for creating different types of plots. All plotting functions expect you to pass data to them and this should be done in the function by use of parameters.

To label, the x and y-axis, use the *plot.xlabel* and *plot.ylabel* respectively.

To label the x and y-axis observation tick points, use *plt.xticks* and *plt.yticks* methods respectively.

Use *plot.legend()* to signify the observation variables.

To set the title of your plot, use the *plot.title()* method.

Display the plot by calling the *plot.show()* method.

Let us demonstrate this by creating a basic chart. As you know, we need data to use for creating the plot. We will use the numpy library so as to create the numbers that we will use to generate the plot. After feeding the data, we will call the *pyplot* module of the matplotlib library to generate the plot. Here is the Python code for this:

```python
import numpy as np
import matplotlib.pyplot as plt

x = np.arange(0,10)
y = x ^ 2
#create and show the Plot
plt.plot(x,y)
plt.show()
```

The code should generate the following plot:

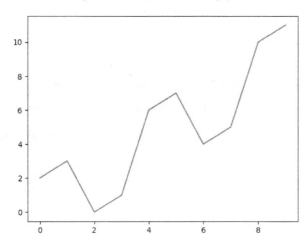

The plot has been created, but one thing you noticed, the axes have not been labelled. Let us label the axes and at the same time, add a title to the chart:

```python
import numpy as np
import matplotlib.pyplot as plt

x = np.arange(0,10)
y = x ^ 2
#Label the Axes and add Title
plt.title("A Graph")
plt.xlabel("X")
plt.ylabel("Y")
#create and show the Plot
plt.plot(x,y)
plt.show()
```

The code should now return the following:

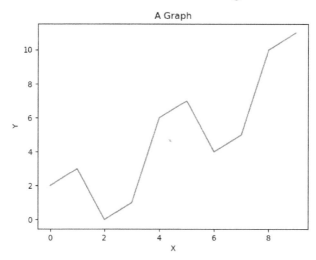

We can also use the appropriate methods to add color to the line as well as the style. This is demonstrated below:

```python
import numpy as np
import matplotlib.pyplot as plt

x = np.arange(0,10)
y = x ^ 2
#Label the Axes and add Title
plt.title("A Graph")
plt.xlabel("X")
plt.ylabel("Y")
# Format the line colors
plt.plot(x,y,'y')
# Format the line type
plt.plot(x,y,'>')
#create and show the Plot
plt.plot(x,y)
plt.show()
```

You should now get the following output:

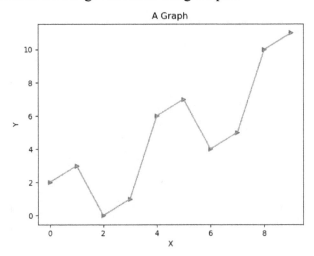

After creating a chart, we can save it by use of various image file formats. The library provides methods for this as shown below:

```python
import numpy as np
import matplotlib.pyplot as plt
```

```
x = np.arange(0,10)
y = x ^ 2
#Label the Axes and add Title
plt.title("A Graph")
plt.xlabel("X")
plt.ylabel("Y")
# Format the line colors
plt.plot(x,y,'y')
# Format the line type
plt.plot(x,y,'>')
#create and show the Plot
plt.plot(x,y)
# save the figure in pdf format
plt.savefig('XvsY.pdf', format='pdf')
plt.show()
```

To confirm whether the pdf file was created or not, open the default path for your Python environment and find the file *XvsY.pdf*. You should find the file with the graph.

Chart Styling

There are methods and libraries that you can use to style your charts. In this section, we will be discussing how to use various properties to style charts in Python:

Adding Annotations

In some cases, we may be in need of annotating the chart by simply highlighting particular locations of the chart. We will demonstrate this by indicating the sharp change in values on the chart by adding annotations to the points. Here is the code for this:

```python
import numpy as np
from matplotlib import pyplot as plt

x = np.arange(0,10)
y = x ^ 2
z = x ^ 3
p = x ^ 4
# Label the Axes and add Title
plt.title("A Graph")
plt.xlabel("X")
plt.ylabel("Y")
plt.plot(x,y)

#Annotate
plt.annotate(xy=[2,1], s='Second Entry')
plt.annotate(xy=[4,6], s='Third Entry')
plt.show()
```

The code should return the following graph:

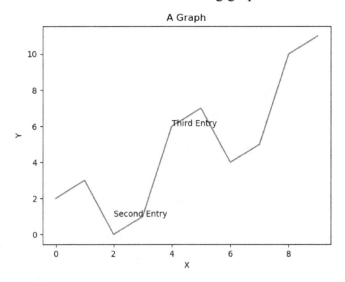

The annotations have been added to the specified points on the chart.

Adding Legends

We sometimes need to have a chart with multiple plotted lines. The use of a legend can help us represent the meaning that is associated with every line. Consider the example given below:

```python
import numpy as np
from matplotlib import pyplot as plt

x = np.arange(0,10)
y = x ^ 2
z = x ^ 3
p = x ^ 4
# Label the Axes and add Title
plt.title("A Graph")
plt.xlabel("X")
plt.ylabel("Y")
plt.plot(x,y)

#Annotate
plt.annotate(xy=[2,1], s='Second Entry')
plt.annotate(xy=[4,6], s='Third Entry')

# Add Legends
plt.plot(x,z)
plt.plot(x,p)
plt.legend(['First set', 'Second set','Third set'], loc=4)

plt.show()
```

The code should return the following chart:

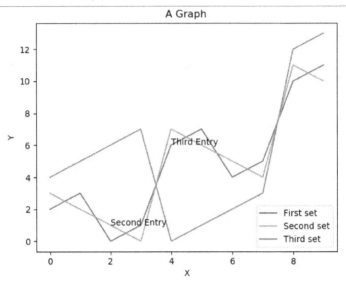

Presentation Style

There are different ways of presenting a chart. The library provides us with numerous methods that we can use to present a chart. The following code demonstrates this:

```python
import numpy as np
from matplotlib import pyplot as plt

x = np.arange(0,10)
y = x ^ 2
z = x ^ 3
p = x ^ 4
# Label the Axes and add Title
plt.title("A Graph")
plt.xlabel("X")
plt.ylabel("Y")
plt.plot(x,y)

#Annotate
```

```
plt.annotate(xy=[2,1], s='Second Entry')
plt.annotate(xy=[4,6], s='Third Entry')

# Add Legends
plt.plot(x,z)
plt.plot(x,p)
plt.legend(['First set', 'Second set','Third
set'], loc=4)

#Styling the background
plt.style.use('fast')
plt.plot(x,z)

plt.show()
```

The code should return the following:

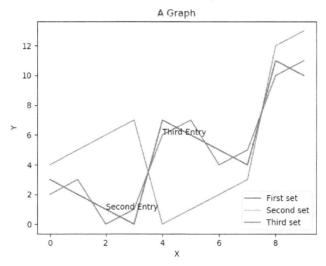

We have used a presentation style known as *fast*. To add this, we called the *plt.style.use()* method.

Line Plot

This is a very basic plot provided by the Matplotlib library.

We can use it to plot any type of function. The line plot shows the series of data points by connecting them using a straight line. We can use a line plot to understand the trend of data over time. The line plot can help in showing the correlation between data points by the trend.

An upward trend will be an indication of a positive correlation while a downward trend will be an indication of a negative correlation. It is widely applied in monitoring and forecasting models. It should be used when you need to plot single or multiple variables over time.

Consider the Python script given below:

```python
import matplotlib.pyplot as plt
import numpy as np

x = np.linspace(-12, 9, 22)

y = x ** 3

plt.plot(x, y, 'b')
plt.xlabel('X')
plt.ylabel('Y')
plt.title('Line Plot')
plt.show()
```

The code returns the following plot:

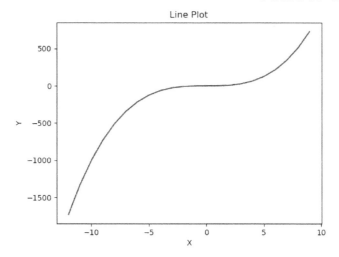

We began by importing the *pyplot* module from Matplotlib and the numpy library. Note that you must have installed the numpy library in your computer for the above code to run successfully. If not, run the following command from the command prompt of your operating system:

```
pip3 install numpy
```

We have then created two numpy arrays, x, and y. We have called the *linspace* method provided by numpy to create a list of numbers between -12 and 9. The cube roots of these numbers have been calculated and the result assigned to variable *y*.

To generate a line plot from the two numpy arrays, we passed them to the *plot* method of the pyplot module. The axis has been labelled and a title assigns to the plot using the necessary libraries.

Here is another example:

```
# Generating a line plot
```

```python
from numpy import sin
from matplotlib import pyplot
# A consistent interval for the x-axis
a = [a*0.1 for a in range(40)]
# function of a for y-axis
b = sin(a)
# Generate the line plot
pyplot.plot(a, b)
# display line plot
pyplot.show()
```

What we have done is that we have created a sequence of 40 floating point values for the x-axis and a sine wave function for the x-axis as y-axis. The code gives the line plot given below:

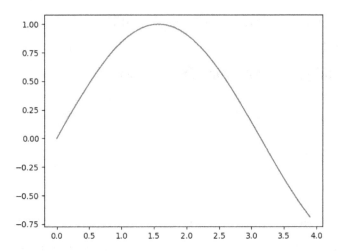

Multiple Plots

With Matplotlib, you can create more than one plot on the same canvas. You do so by use of the *subplot()* function which defines the location and the number of the plot. Consider the example given below:

```
import numpy as np
import matplotlib.pyplot as plt

x = np.linspace(-12, 9, 22)

y = x ** 3

plt.subplot(2,2,1)
plt.plot(x, y, 'b*-')
plt.subplot(2,2,2)
plt.plot(x, y, 'y--')
plt.subplot(2,2,3)
plt.plot(x, y, 'b*-')
plt.subplot(2,2,4)
plt.plot(x, y, 'y--')
plt.show()
```

The code will return the following when executed:

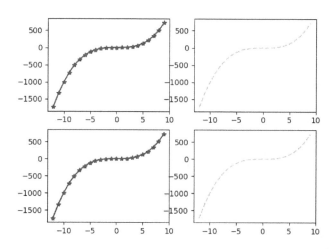

The first attribute passed to the *subplot* function defines the rows that the subplot will have while the second parameter denotes the number of columns to be used in the subplot. When we use a

value of (2, 2), it states that there will be 4 graphs. The third
parameter specifies the position for the display of the graph. These
positions begin from top-left. A plot with a position of 1 will be
displayed in row 1 and column 1. A plot with a position of 2 will
be displayed in row 1 column 2.

The third parameter of the *plot* function defines the color and
shape of the marker on the graph.

In the previous example, we used the *plot* function of the
pyplot module and passed the values of x and y coordinates
together with the labels. However, we can achieve the same by use
of an object-oriented approach. Consider the script given below:

```python
import matplotlib.pyplot as plt
import numpy as np

x = np.linspace(-12, 9, 22)

y = x ** 3

fig = plt.figure()

axes = fig.add_axes([0.2, 0.2, 0.8, 0.8])
plt.show()
```

Note that we have called the *figure()* method by use of the
pyplot class. To return the *fig* object. We have then used this object
to call the *add_axes()* method. Note that we have passed some
parameters to the *add_axes()* method. These specify the distance
from the left and the bottom of the default axis and the width and
height of the axis, respectively. The values of the parameters
should be added as a fraction of the default size of the figure.

We can now add the data labels to the axis. The data can be

passed to the *plot* function. We will also set the labels for the axis and add the title. This is demonstrated below:

```python
import matplotlib.pyplot as plt
import numpy as np

x = np.linspace(-12, 9, 22)

y = x ** 3

fig = plt.figure()

axes = fig.add_axes([0.2, 0.2, 0.8, 0.8])

axes.plot(x, y, 'b')
axes.set_xlabel('X')
axes.set_ylabel('Y')
axes.set_title('A Chart')

plt.show()
```

You will get a similar plot as the previous one but we have used an object-oriented approach.

Stack Plot

This is an advanced line chart or bar chart that breaks down data from various categories and stacks them together so that a comparison between the values from various categories may be made.

Suppose you need to compare the class points scored by three different students per year over the last 8 years. You can use the Matplotlib to create a stack plot as shown below:

```python
import matplotlib.pyplot as plt

year = [2011, 2012, 2013, 2014, 2015, 2016,
2017, 2018]

student1 = [8,10,17,15,23,18,24,29]
student2 = [10,14,19,16,25,20,26,32]
student3 = [12,17,21,19,26,22,28,35]

plt.plot([],[], color='y', label =
'student1')
plt.plot([],[], color='r', label =
'student2')
plt.plot([],[], color='b', label = 'student3
')

plt.stackplot(year, student1, student2,
student3, colors = ['r','g','y'])
plt.legend()
plt.title('Students Marks')
plt.xlabel('year')
plt.ylabel('Marks')
plt.show()
```

The code will return the following plot:

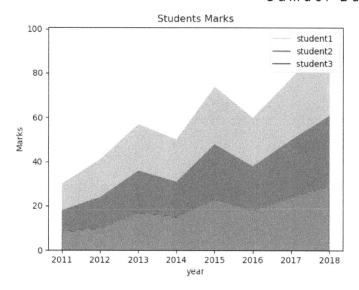

We simply called the *stackplt* function provided by the Matplotlib library. The values to be displayed should be passed as the first parameter to the class while the values that are to be stacked on the horizontal axis will be displayed as the second parameter, third parameter, etc. You can use the *color* attribute to set the color of every category.

P i e   C h a r t

This is a circular plot that has been divided into slices illustrating numerical proportions. Every slice in the pie chart shows the proportion of the element to the whole. A large category means that it will occupy a larger portion of the pie chart.

The following example demonstrates this:

```python
import matplotlib.pyplot as plt

students = 'John', 'Mercy', 'Boss'
```

```
points = [62,48,36]
colors = ['y','r','b']

plt.pie(points, labels = students,
colors=colors ,shadow = True, explode =
(0.05, 0.05, 0.05), autopct = '%1.1f%%')
plt.axis('equal')

plt.show()
```

The code will return the following chart:

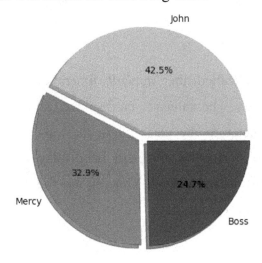

To create a pie chart, we call the *pie* method of the pyplot module. The first parameter to the method is the list of numbers for every category. A list of categories separated by commas is then passed as the argument to *labels* attribute. The list of colors for every category is then passed as arguments to the *colors* attribute. If you set the *shadow* attribute to *true*, it will create shadows around the various categories on your pie chart. Finally, the use of the *explode* attribute will split each slice of the pie chart into its

Histogram

When creating a histogram, it takes a series of data then it subdivides the data into a number of bins. The frequency data points are then plotted on every bin, that is, the interval of the points. It is a good tool when you need to understand the count of data ranges.

It is recommended you use a histogram when you need to get the count of the variable in a plot. The following code demonstrates how to plot a histogram:

```python
import matplotlib.pyplot as plt
import numpy as np
np.set_printoptions(precision=3)

data = np.random.laplace(loc=15, scale=3,
size=400)
data[:5]

n, bins, patches = plt.hist(x=data,
bins='auto', color='#0504aa',
                            alpha=0.75,
rwidth=0.90)
plt.grid(axis='y', alpha=0.80)
plt.xlabel('Value')
plt.ylabel('Frequency')
plt.title('Histogram')
plt.text(23, 45, r'$\mu=15, b=3$')
maxfreq = n.max()

plt.ylim(ymax=np.ceil(maxfreq / 10) * 10 if
maxfreq % 10 else maxfreq + 10)
plt.show()
```

The code will return the following plot:

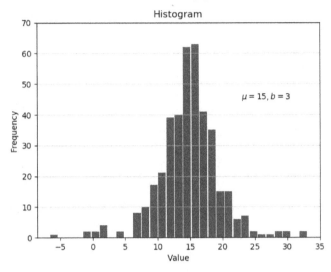

We create a histogram by calling the *pyplot.hist()* method. It expects an array as the parameter and the number of expected bins can be specified. The plot of the histogram will use the bin edges on the x-axis and corresponding frequencies on y-axis. The use of *bins= 'auto'* in the above code facilitates choosing between two algorithms to estimate the number of bins. For the case of a high level, the algorithm aims at choosing a bin width that will generate the most faithful representation of data.

Here is another example:

```
# Generating a histogram plot
from numpy.random import seed
from numpy.random import randn
from matplotlib import pyplot
# seed a random number generator
seed(1)
# To get random numbers from Gaussian
distribution
a = randn(200)
```

```
# Generate  histogram plot
pyplot.hist(a)
# show line plot
pyplot.show()
```

In the above example, we have created a dataset of 200 random numbers that have been drawn from a Gaussian distribution. The dataset has then been plotted into a histogram. The code generates the following histogram:

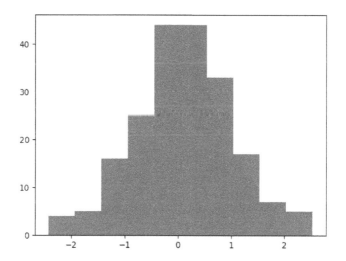

It is recommended that one should be kept when choosing the number of bins. This way, it will be easy for them to tell the shape of the distribution of the data.

Scatter Plot

This is a type of plot that shows many data points plotted on a cartesian plane. Each point on the Cartesian plane is a representation of two variables. One of the variables is chosen on the vertical axis while the other one is chosen on the horizontal axis.

To create a scatter plot, we call the *scatter()* method of pyplot
module. This method takes two numeric data points for scattering
the data points on the plot. See it as a line plot without the
connection straight line. The following example demonstrates how
to create a scatter plot:

```python
import numpy as np
import pandas as pd
import matplotlib.pyplot as plt
# Create the data
N = 100
x = np.random.rand(N)
y = np.random.rand(N)
colors = (0,100,255)
area = np.pi*3
# Generate the plot
plt.scatter(x, y)
plt.title('A Scatter Plot')
plt.xlabel('x')
plt.ylabel('y')
plt.show()
```

The code should return the following scatter plot:

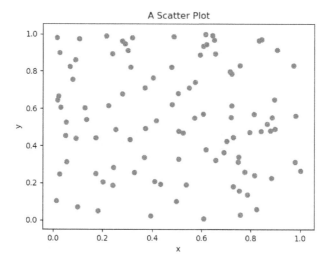

Here is another example:

```
# Creating a scatter plot
from numpy.random import seed
from numpy.random import randn
from matplotlib import pyplot
# seed a random number generator
seed(1)
# create the first variable
a = 20 * randn(200) + 50
# create the second variable
b = a + (10 * randn(200) + 100)
# generate a scatter plot
pyplot.scatter(a, b)
# display line plot
pyplot.show()
```

We began by creating two related data samples. The first sample was generated from a Gaussian distribution. The second sample relies on the first sample and is obtained by adding the second random Gaussian value to the value of first measure. The code generates the following once executed:

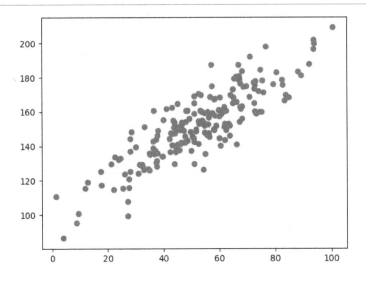

Box Plots

Box plots help us measure how well data in a dataset is distributed. The dataset is divided into three quartiles. The graph shows the maximum, minimum, median, first quartile and third quartiles of the dataset. It is also good for comparing how data is distributed across datasets by creating box plots for each dataset.

Use a boxplot when you need to get the overall statistical information about the data distribution. It is a good tool for detecting outliers in a dataset.

To create a boxplot, we call the *boxplot* method of pyplot. The method takes the name of the dataset as the parameter. Consider the example given below:

```
import matplotlib.pyplot as plt

student1 = [8,10,17,15,23,18,24,29]
student2 = [10,14,19,16,25,20,26,32]
student3 = [12,17,21,19,26,22,28,35]
```

```
data=[student1, student2, student3]
plt.boxplot(data)
plt.show()
```

The code should return the following box plot:

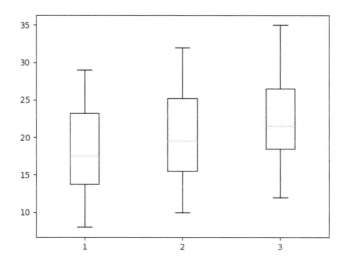

What we have done is that we passed three arrays to an array named *data*. We have then passed the name of this array to the *boxplot* function.

The line dividing the box into two shows the median of the data. The end of the box represents the upper quartile (75%) while the start of the box represents the lower quartile (25%). In some cases, the upper quartile is referred to as the 3rd quartile while the lower quartile is referred to as the 1st quartile. The part between the upper quartile and the lower quartile is known as the *Inter Quartile Range* (IQR) and helps in approximating 50% of the middle data.

The end of the upper whisker shows the maximum value in the data while the end of the lower whisker shows the minimum value in the data. Any points shown on the extremes represent the outliers in the data.

Here is another example:

```
# Creating a box and whisker plot
from numpy.random import seed
from numpy.random import randn
from matplotlib import pyplot
# seed a random number generator
seed(1)
# random numbers obtained from Gaussian
distribution
a = [randn(300), 5 * randn(300), 10 *
randn(300)]
# generate the box and whisker plot
pyplot.boxplot(a)
# display line plot
pyplot.show()
```

In the above example, we are creating three box plots in a single chart. Each of these summarizes a data sample that has been obtained from different Gaussian distributions. Each data sample is created in the form of an array, and the three arrays are added into a list which is in turn passed to a plotting function. The code generates the following once executed:

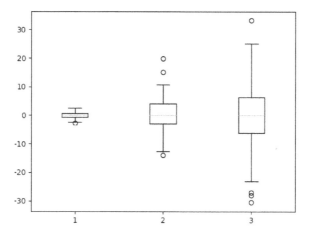

The chart has three box and whisker plots. A similar scale has been used for these for the y-axis. The black box represents the middle of the data, which is 50%. The orange line represents the median while the box and whisker lines give a summary of the sensible data. The dots show any outliers in your data.

B a r   C h a r t

This type of chart is used for showing the distribution of data over many groups. Most people confuse it with the histogram but note that a histogram only accepts numerical data for plotting. It is only good for comparing numerical values. Use a bar plot when you need to make a comparison between multiple groups.

To create a bar plot, we use the *bar* method of the *Matplotlib* library. The following example demonstrates this:

```python
import matplotlib.pyplot as plt
plt.bar([2,4,5,9,12],[5,1,7,9,3],
label="First Data")
```

```
plt.bar([3,4,7,8,11],[9,6,1,5,7],
label="Second Data", color='g')
plt.legend()
plt.xlabel('Bar number')
plt.ylabel('Bar height')
plt.title('A Bar Graph')
plt.show()
```

The code should return the following bar graph:

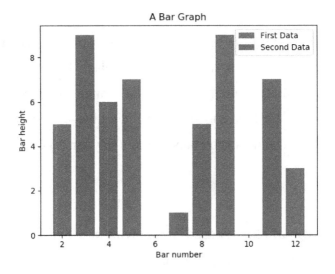

Here is another example:

```
# creating a bar chart
from random import seed
from random import randint
from matplotlib import pyplot
# seed a random number generator
seed(1)
# category names
x = ['Xtrail', 'Rav 4', 'Outlander']
# quantities sold for each category
```

```
y = [randint(0, 100), randint(0, 100),
randint(0, 100)]
# generate the bar chart
pyplot.bar(x, y)
# display the line plot
pyplot.show()
```

We have created three categories namely Xtrail, Rav 4 and Outlander. A single random integer has been drawn to represent the value of each category. The code generated the bar chart shown below:

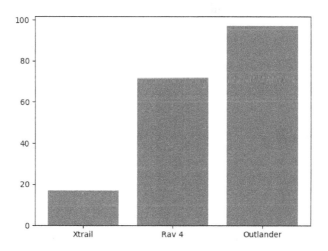

Bubble Chart

This type of chart shows the data in the form of a cluster of circles. The data to generate the bubble chart should have the xy coordinates, the bubble size and the color of the bubbles. The colors can be supplied by use of the Matplotlib library.

To create a bubble chart, we use the *scatter* method provided in the Matplotlib library. Here is an example:

```python
import numpy as np
import matplotlib.pyplot as plt

# create the data
x = np.random.rand(30)
y = np.random.rand(30)
z = np.random.rand(30)
colors = np.random.rand(30)
# scatter function
plt.scatter(x, y, s=z*1000,c=colors)
plt.show()
```

The code will generate the following bubble chart:

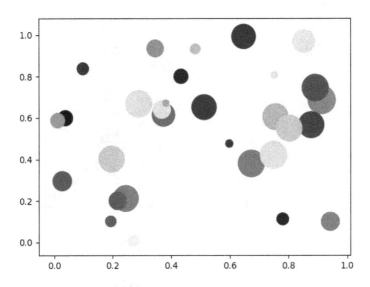

Heat Maps

A heat map has values representing different shades of a similar color for every value that is to be plotted. The darker shades of the chart indicate the higher values compared to the lighter shades. For the case of a very different value, you can use a more different color.

Consider the example given below:

```python
from pandas import DataFrame
import matplotlib.pyplot as plt

data=[{3,4,6,1},{6,5,4,2},{7,3,5,2},{2,7,5,3
},{1,8,1,4}]
Index= ['I1', 'I2','I3','I4','I5']
Cols = ['Col1', 'Col2', 'ol','Col4']
df = DataFrame(data, index=Index,
columns=Cols)

plt.pcolor(df)
plt.show()
```

The code will return the following result:

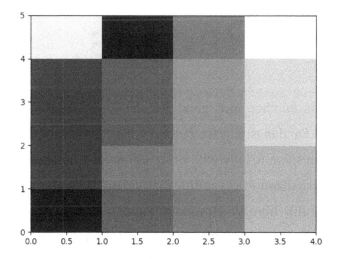

We have created a two-dimensional plot of values that are mapped to the columns and indices of the chart.

6-Data Visualization with Pandas

This is another tool good for data visualization. The good thing with Pandas is that we require a less amount of code so as to achieve the same results with other libraries. You should note that the data visualization capabilities provided by Pandas are based on the Matplotlib library. However, Pandas allows you to directly create plots from its data structures like the dataframe.

Let us discuss the various plots that can be plotted with Pandas:

We will use the Titanic dataset. You can find the dataset from the following URL:

https://www.kaggle.com/c/titanic/data

We will use the *train.csv* dataset. Download the *train.csv* dataset and save it in the directory of your Python scripts.

Now, let us import the required libraries:

```
import numpy as np
import pandas as pd
import matplotlib.pyplot as plt
```

Let us now import the dataset into the work environment by running the following command:

```
titanic_data = pd.read_csv(r"train.csv")
```

The *r* means that the data has been opened for reading. Let us have a look at the dataset:

```
titanic_data.head()
```

The command should return the following result:

```
   PassengerId  Survived  Pclass   ...       Fare  Cabin  Embarked
0            1         0       3    ...     7.2500    NaN         S
1            2         1       1    ...    71.2833    C85         C
2            3         1       3    ...     7.9250    NaN         S
3            4         1       1    ...    53.1000   C123         S
4            5         0       3    ...     8.0500    NaN         S

[5 rows x 12 columns]
```

If it returns an error, it could because it is looking for output information. Just import the *sys* library and the following statement:

```
import sys
sys.__stdout__ = sys.stdout
```

The data has the details of the passengers who lost their lives

in the titanic ship in 1912. We will be using this data to create
various types of plots with the Pandas library.

Histogram

A histogram is also a good tool for data visualization. In
pandas, a histogram can be plotted by calling the *plot.hist()*
method. The following code demonstrates how to plot a histogram
in pandas:

```python
import pandas as pd
import numpy as np
from matplotlib import pyplot
p =
pd.DataFrame({'x':np.random.randn(500)+1,'y'
:np.random.randn(500),'z':
np.random.randn(500) - 1}, columns=['x',
'y', 'z'])

p.plot.hist(bins=20)
pyplot.show()
```

The code will generate the following histogram:

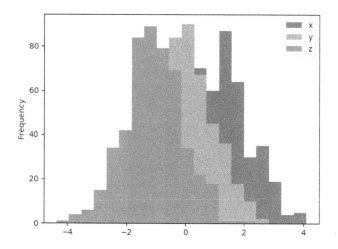

We can also create a histogram from the *train.csv file*. If the histogram is to be plotted from a single column, we only have to specify the name of the column followed by the *hist()* method. Let us plot a histogram for the Age column:

```python
import numpy as np
import pandas as pd
import matplotlib.pyplot as plt
import sys

sys.__stdout__ = sys.stdout

titanic_data = pd.read_csv(r"train.csv")

titanic_data['Age'].hist()
plt.show()
```

The code will return the following result:

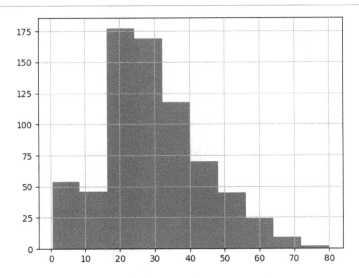

See how easy it was for us to create a histogram for the Age column using the Pandas dataframe.

It is possible for us to pass Matplotlib parameters to the hist() method since the Pandas library is based on Matplotlib. For instance, we can use the *bin* attribute to increase the ethe number of bins. This is shown below:

```
titanic_data['Age'].hist(bins=20)
```

The code should now be as follows:

```
import numpy as np
import pandas as pd
import matplotlib.pyplot as plt
import sys

sys.__stdout__ = sys.stdout

titanic_data = pd.read_csv(r"train.csv")
```

```
titanic_data['Age'].hist(bins=20)
plt.show()
```

The code should return the following histogram:

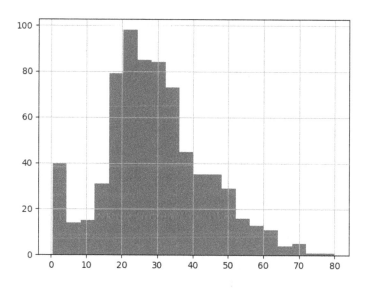

The number of bins was set to 20. We can improve the style of our Histogram by importing the Seaborn library then we set a value for the *set_style* attribute. Let us use a dark gray grid by adding the following command:

First, we import the Seaborn library:

```
import seaborn as sns
```

Now, we can add the following command:

```
sns.set_style('darkgrid')
```

So that the code becomes:

```python
import numpy as np
import pandas as pd
import matplotlib.pyplot as plt
import sys
import seaborn as sns


sys.__stdout__ = sys.stdout

titanic_data = pd.read_csv(r"train.csv")

titanic_data['Age'].hist(bins=20)
sns.set_style('darkgrid')
plt.show()
```

The code returns the following:

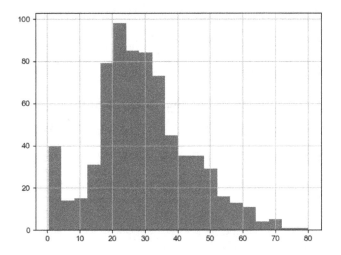

There are two ways through which a data frame can be used for plotting graphs. The first way is passing a value for the *kind* parameter of the plot function. This is shown below:

```
titanic_data['Age'].plot(kind='hist',
bins=20)
```

So that the entire code is as follows:

```
import numpy as np
import pandas as pd
import matplotlib.pyplot as plt
import sys
import seaborn as sns


sys.__stdout__ = sys.stdout

titanic_data = pd.read_csv(r"train.csv")
titanic_data['Age'].plot(kind='hist',
bins=20)


sns.set_style('darkgrid')
plt.show()
```

Which returns the following histogram?

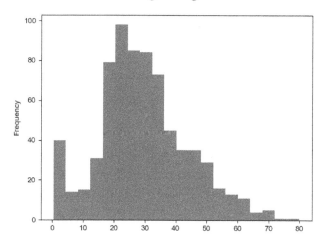

The second way involves calling the method name directly by use of the *plot* function without having to pass the name of the function to the *kind* attribute.

Line Plot

A line plot can be created in the Pandas library by calling the *line()* method using the *plot* function and passing to it the value of x-index and y-axis. The following statement describes this:

```
titanic_data.plot.line(x='Age', y='Fare',
figsize=(8,6))
```

You should have the following as the complete code for this:

```
import numpy as np
import pandas as pd
import matplotlib.pyplot as plt
import sys

sys.__stdout__ = sys.stdout

titanic_data = pd.read_csv(r"train.csv")
titanic_data.plot.line(x='Age', y='Fare',
figsize=(8,6))
plt.show()
```

The above script will create a line plot with the x-axis being the age of the passengers while the y-axis will have the fares paid by the passengers. The *figsize* has helped us in changing the size of our plot. The script should return the following output:

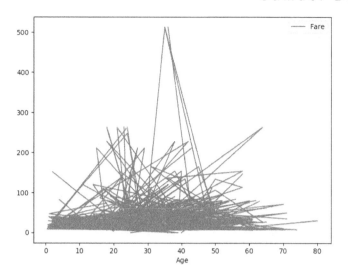

Scatter Plot

To create a scatterplot, we call the *DataFrame.plot.scatter()* method. Here is a simple example:

```
import pandas as pd
import numpy as np
from matplotlib import pyplot
df = pd.DataFrame(np.random.rand(40, 5),
columns=['v', 'w', 'x', 'y', 'z'])
df.plot.scatter(x='v', y='w')
pyplot.show()
```

The code generates the plot given below:

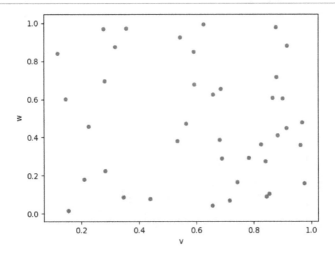

On the y-axis, we have w while on the x-axis we have v. The data points are shown in the way they are distributed on the plot.

For the case of our *train.csv* dataset, we can plot a scatter plot by running the following command:

```
titanic_data.plot.scatter(x='Age', y='Fare',
figsize=(8,6))
```

So that your complete code is as follows:

```
import numpy as np
import pandas as pd
import matplotlib.pyplot as plt
import sys


sys.__stdout__ = sys.stdout

titanic_data = pd.read_csv(r"train.csv")
titanic_data.plot.scatter(x='Age', y='Fare',
figsize=(8,6))
plt.show()
```

The code should return the following result:

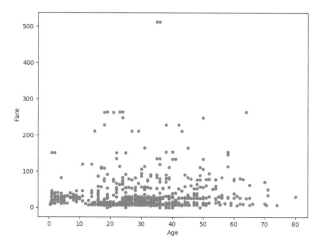

To create a box plot with pandas, we call *box()* method to show how the values are distributed within every column. Consider the following example:

```
import pandas as pd
import numpy as np
from matplotlib import pyplot
df = pd.DataFrame(np.random.rand(10, 5),
columns=['V', 'W', 'X', 'Y', 'Z'])
df.plot.box()
pyplot.show()
```

The above code helps us draw a box plot of 10 observations for 5 trials for a uniform random variable. The code generates the following boxplot:

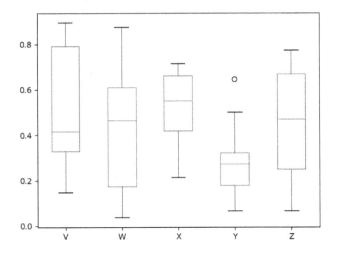

We can still use the *train.csv* dataset to create a box plot. We will still use the *box()* method using the *plot* function provided by the Pandas data frame. You should use the following line of code:

```
titanic_data.plot.box(figsize=(10,8))
```

Your entire code should be as follows:

```
import numpy as np
import pandas as pd
import matplotlib.pyplot as plt
import sys

sys.__stdout__ = sys.stdout

titanic_data = pd.read_csv(r"train.csv")
titanic_data.plot.box(figsize=(10,8))
plt.show()
```

The code should return the following plot:

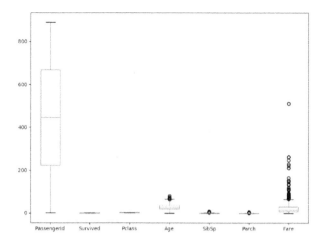

There are box plots for all the numeric columns contained in the dataset.

H e x a g o n a l   P l o t s

The purpose of hexagonal plots is to create hexagons that will intersect the data points on the x and y-axis. A high number of intersecting points means a darker hexagon. To create a hexagon from the Pandas dataframe, use the *plot* function to call the *hexbin()* method. The values for the x-index and y-axis should be passed. This is demonstrated below:

```
titanic_data.plot.hexbin(x='Age', y='Fare',
gridsize=30, figsize=(8,6))
```

So that your entire code is as follows:

```
import numpy as np
import pandas as pd
import matplotlib.pyplot as plt
import sys
```

```
sys.__stdout__ = sys.stdout

titanic_data = pd.read_csv(r"train.csv")
titanic_data.plot.hexbin(x='Age', y='Fare',
gridsize=30, figsize=(8,6))

plt.show()
```

To return the following hexagon:

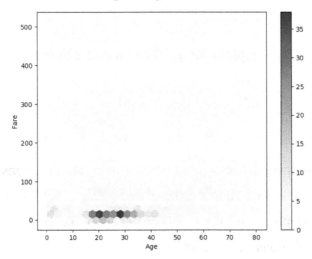

Kernel Density Plots

It is possible for us to draw a kernel density plot using the Pandas library. You only have to use the *plot* function to call the *kde()* method as demonstrated below:

```
titanic_data['Age'].plot.kde()
```

You should now have the following code:

```
import numpy as np
import pandas as pd
import matplotlib.pyplot as plt
import sys

sys.__stdout__ = sys.stdout

titanic_data = pd.read_csv(r"train.csv")
titanic_data['Age'].plot.kde()

plt.show()
```

The code should return the following plot:

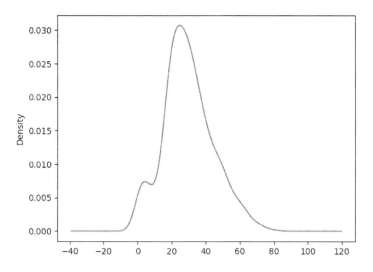

Area Plot

To create an area plot, we need to call either *Series.plot.area()* or

DataFrame.plot.area() methods. This is demonstrated below:

```
import pandas as pd
import numpy as np
```

```
from matplotlib import pyplot
a = pd.DataFrame(np.random.rand(15, 4),
columns=['v', 'w', 'x', 'y'])
a.plot.area()
pyplot.show()
```

The generated area plot will be as shown below:

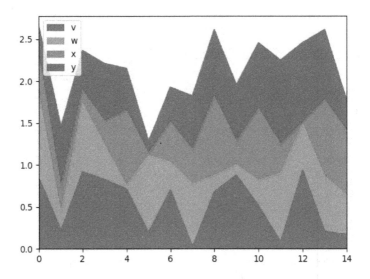

Pie Chart

A pie chart is a good way of showing the value contributed by a certain variable by the total contributed by all variables. It provides us with a way of comparing the values of different variables in a dataset. Consider the following example:

```
import pandas as pd
import numpy as np
from matplotlib import pyplot
```

```
p = pd.DataFrame(3 * np.random.rand(4),
index=['w', 'x', 'y', 'z'], columns=[''])
p.plot.pie(subplots=True)
pyplot.show()
```

The code will generate the following pie chart when executed:

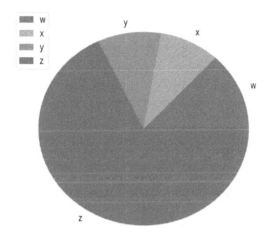

From the above pie chart, it is clear that z has the highest contribution, followed by w. The contributions made by x and y to the dataset are almost equal.

Bar plot

A bar plot can also help you see the variable with the greatest contribution in a dataset. The individual contribution of each variable is plotted in terms of a bar and the size of the bar corresponds to the individual contribution of the variable. The following code demonstrates how to plot a bar graph with pandas:

```
import pandas as pd
```

```
import numpy as np
from matplotlib import pyplot
p = pd.DataFrame(3 * np.random.rand(4),
index=['w', 'x', 'y', 'z'])
p.plot.bar()
pyplot.show()
```

The code will generate the following bar chart once executed:

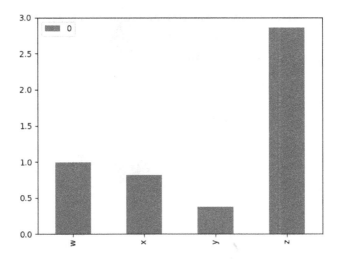

The bar plot shows z has the largest contribution, followed by w, x and lastly y. This means y has the smallest contribution.

If you need to have bars that run horizontally, use the *barh(stacked=True)* method. This is shown in the following code:

```
import pandas as pd
import numpy as np
from matplotlib import pyplot
p = pd.DataFrame(3 * np.random.rand(4),
index=['w', 'x', 'y', 'z'])
p.plot.barh(stacked=True)
pyplot.show()
```

To return the following chart:

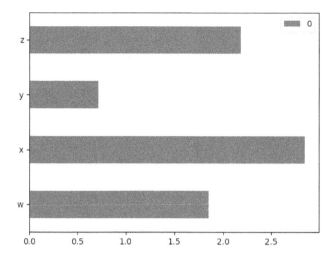

Time Series

A time series data is the kind of data in which the features or attributes depend on a time index which is also a dataset feature. Examples of time series data include the number of items sold per hour, daily stock prices and daily temperatures. In these types of data, the data depends on a time unit and it varies depending on that time unit. The time series could be an hour, a day, a week, a month, a year, etc.

The Pandas library is a good tool for visualizing time series data. The library comes with numerous built-in functions that can help in performing a number of tasks related to time series data such as time sampling and shifting.

Our first step should be to get the time series data. As we had stated, an example of a time series data is the stock price data that varies over a period of time. We will use the APL stock price data which can be downloaded by clicking Yahoo Finance section of the website, that is, https://finance.yahoo.com. The file with the

data is given the name AAPL.csv, meaning that the data is in a
CSV format.

Let us begin by importing the libraries that we will need in the
plotting of the time series data:

```python
import pandas as pd
import numpy as np

%matplotlib inline
import matplotlib.pyplot as plt
```

Next, we can call the *read_csv()* method provided by the
Pandas library. This can be done as follows:

```python
data = pd.read_csv(r'AAPL.csv')
```

Let us now call the *head()* function to see how the data looks
like:

```python
data.head()
```

You should the following code so far:

```python
import pandas as pd
import numpy as np

%matplotlib inline
import matplotlib.pyplot as plt

data = pd.read_csv(r'AAPL.csv')
print(data.head())
```

It returns the following:

```
        Date      Open       High      ...      Close  Adj Close   Volume
0  2013-12-10  80.511429  81.125717    ...   80.792854  72.922142  69567400
1  2013-12-11  81.000000  81.567146    ...   80.194283  72.381866  59929700
2  2013-12-12  80.305717  80.762856    ...   80.077141  72.276154  65572500
3  2013-12-13  80.407143  80.411430    ...   79.204285  71.488319  83205500
4  2013-12-16  79.288574  80.377144    ...   79.642860  71.884155  70648200

[5 rows x 7 columns]
```

As you can see, the data is about stock prices. It has the date, the opening and the closing price of the stock for the day, the adjusted close price and the stock volume. It is clear that all the columns depend on the date. A change in the date column causes a change in the other columns. This means that the Date column forms the index for the data. However, in this dataset, the date is treated as a string.

This means that we should change this from the String data type to the DateTime data type and set it as the index column. The following code will help you change the column data type from a string to DateTime:

```
data['Date'] =
data['Date'].apply(pd.to_datetime)
```

What we have done in the above line is that we have applied the *to_datetime* function on the Date column so as to change the data type. To set the Date column as the index, run the following script:

```
data.set_index('Date', inplace=True)
```

We have only called the *set_index* method and passed the name of the column to it as the parameter. The use of the *inPlace=True* attribute means that the conversion will happen in a place and there will be no need for you to store the result into

another variable. We can now use the *head()* function to see the
first 5 rows of our dataset:

```
data.head()
```

The whole code should now be as follows:

```python
import pandas as pd
import numpy as np

import matplotlib.pyplot as plt
import sys

sys.__stdout__ = sys.stdout

data = pd.read_csv(r'AAPL.csv')
data['Date'] =
data['Date'].apply(pd.to_datetime)
data.set_index('Date', inplace=True)
print(data.head())
```

The code should return the following result:

```
                Open        High     ...    Adj Close    Volume
Date                                 ...
2013-12-10    80.511429   81.125717  ...    72.922142   69567400
2013-12-11    81.000000   81.567146  ...    72.381866   89929700
2013-12-12    80.305717   80.762856  ...    72.276154   65572500
2013-12-13    80.407143   80.411430  ...    71.488319   83205500
2013-12-16    79.288574   80.377144  ...    71.884155   70648200

[5 rows x 6 columns]
```

We can now plot the closing price of the Apple stock before
we can proceed to shift:

```
data["Close"].plot(grid=True)
plt.show()
```

The code should return the following output:

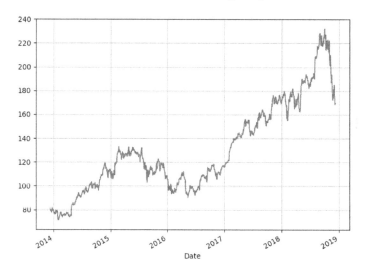

See that we have simply called the *plot* function on the Close column of the dataset. No information has been specified about the date, but since we set the Date column as the index for the data, its values will be plotted on the x-axis while the values for the closing column will be plotted on the y-axis.

There are a number of visualization tasks that Pandas can perform on time series data. Examples include Time shifting and Time sampling.

Time Shifting

Time shifting is the process of moving your data some steps either forward or backward. It is one of the major tasks in time series analysis. You saw the head of the dataset previously. We now want to have a look at the tail of the dataset. The dataframes of the head and the tail will later be used for the purpose of observing the effects of time shifting.

To see the tail of the dataset, we call the *tail()* method as shown below:

```
data.tail()
```

The code returns the following output:

```
>>> data.tail()
                  Open        High     ...    Adj Close    Volume
Date                                   ...
2018-12-03   184.460007  184.940002   ...   182.630859   40802500
2018-12-04   180.949997  182.389999   ...   174.597153   41344300
2018-12-06   171.759995  174.779999   ...   172.650482   43098400
2018-12-07   173.490005  174.490005   ...   166.494278   42281600
2018-12-10   165.000000  170.089996   ...   167.591125   62026000

[5 rows x 6 columns]
>>>
```

We will first move our data forward and see the way time-shifting works in a positive direction. If you need to move your data a certain number of steps forward, just call the *shift()* method on the data then pass to it an integer argument. The integer specifies the number of times or steps to move the data.

Consider the example given below:

```
data.shift(2).head()
```

In the above script, we are shifting the data two steps forward and printing the head of the data. It prints the following output:

```
>>> data.shift(2).head()
                 Open        High     ...    Adj Close      Volume
Date                                  ...
2013-12-10        NaN         NaN     ...          NaN         NaN
2013-12-11        NaN         NaN     ...          NaN         NaN
2013-12-12   80.511429   81.125717    ...    72.922142  69567400.0
2013-12-13   81.000000   81.567146    ...    72.381866  89929700.0
2013-12-16   80.305717   80.762856    ...    72.276154  65572500.0

[5 rows x 6 columns]
>>>
```

In the above output, you realize that no data has been printed for the first two rows of the dataset as the data for the rows has been moved 2 steps forward.

If you need to shift the data negative, just call the *shift()* function and pass to it a negative integer value. For example, if your goal is to shift the data two steps backwards, run the following script:

```
data.shift(-2).tail()
```

The script returns the following:

```
>>> data.shift(-2).tail()
                  Open         High     ...    Adj Close      Volume
Date                                    ...
2018-12-03  171.759995   174.779999    ...    172.650482  43098400.0
2018-12-04  173.490005   174.490005    ...    166.494278  42281600.0
2018-12-06  165.000000   170.089996    ...    167.591125  62026000.0
2018-12-07         NaN          NaN    ...           NaN         NaN
2018-12-10         NaN          NaN    ...           NaN         NaN

[5 rows x 6 columns]
>>>
```

The script shifted the data two steps backward and then displayed the tail of the dataset. The output shows that there are no records for the last two rows since the data has been moved two steps back.

Time   Sampling

This is the process of grouping the attributes and features of your data depending on the aggregated value of the index column. A good example is when you need to see the overall maximum opening stock price per year for all years in the dataset. This is a good scenario for you to use time sampling.

It is easy for us to implement time sampling in Pandas. You only have to call the *resample()* method by use of the Pandas dataframe. The value should also be passed for the *rule* attribute. This value is for the time-offset that specifies the time frame for which we need to group the data.

Finally, we can call the aggregation functions such as *min, max, mean, etc.* Consider the example given below:

```
data.resample(rule='M').max()
```

The above script will show the maximum value for all the attributes for every month in the dataset. Here is a section of the output from the script:

```
>>> data.resample(rule='M').max()
                 Open        High     ...     Adj Close     Volume
Date                                  ...
2013-12-31    81.412857    81.697144  ...     73.507507   141465800
2014-01-31    79.382858    80.028572  ...     71.866127   266380800
2014-02-28    78.000000    78.741432  ...     70.821465   100366000
2014-03-31    78.074287    78.428574  ...     70.691750    93511600
2014-04-30    84.820000    85.632858  ...     77.060608   189977900
2014-05-31    91.139999    92.024284  ...     82.876732   141005200
2014-06-30    94.730003    95.050003  ...     86.055473   100898000
2014-07-31    99.330002    99.440002  ...     90.410744    92918000
2014-08-31   102.860002   102.900002  ...     94.053680    69399000
2014-09-30   103.099998   103.739998  ...     94.787781   189846300
2014-10-31   108.010002   108.040001  ...     99.100471   100933600
2014-11-30   119.269997   119.750000  ...    109.667534    68840400
2014-12-31   118.809998   119.250000  ...    106.838287    88429800
2015-01-31   118.400002   120.000000  ...    109.575378   146477100
2015-02-28   132.940002   133.600006  ...    123.053322    91287500
2015-03-31   129.250000   130.279999  ...    119.685532    88528500
2015-04-30   134.460007   134.539993  ...    122.729507   118924000
2015-05-31   132.600006   132.970001  ...    123.139961    72141000
2015-06-30   130.660004   131.389999  ...    121.281799    56075400
2015-07-31   132.850006   132.970001  ...    122.703278   115450600
2015-08-31   121.500000   122.570000  ...    111.732651   162206300
2015-09-30   116.580002   116.889999  ...    108.643478    85010800
2015-10-31   120.989998   121.220001  ...    112.488594    85551400
2015-11-30   123.129997   123.820000  ...    114.392502    59127900
2015-12-31   118.980003   119.860001  ...    111.564194    96453300
2016-01-31   105.750000   105.849998  ...     98.742249   133369700
2016-02-29    98.839996    98.889999  ...     92.464752    54021400
2016-03-31   109.720001   110.419998  ...    103.245384    50407100
2016-04-30   112.110001   112.389999  ...    105.638985   114602100
2016-05-31    99.680000   100.730003  ...     95.198868    76314700
 ...             ...          ...     ...        ...          ...
```

We can now print the average quarterly values (for every three months) for the dataset. We will use Q which represents the quarterly frequency. Just run the script given below:

```
data.resample(rule='Q').mean()
```

It returns the following:

```
>>> data.resample(rule='Q').mean()
                Open        High      ...    Adj Close        Volume
                                      ...
Date
2013-12-31   79.928287    80.381809  ...    71.999433   7.739415e+07
2014-03-31   76.099017    76.697822  ...    68.923138   8.052467e+07
2014-06-30   84.989161    85.653084  ...    77.552178   6.745424e+07
2014-09-30   98.127500    98.958125  ...    89.898093   5.466536e+07
2014-12-31  108.795000   109.861875  ...   100.121296   5.084817e+07
2015-03-31  120.999836   122.056230  ...   111.591276   5.869575e+07
2015-06-30  128.074445   128.968889  ...   118.669254   4.490308e+07
2015-09-30  117.428125   118.755156  ...   109.273228   6.049448e+07
2015-12-31  114.362656   115.356563  ...   106.951786   4.351669e+07
2016-03-31   99.562459   100.677541  ...    93.731477   4.637312e+07
2016-06-30   99.399688   100.266250  ...    94.016147   3.988364e+07
2016-09-30  105.700156   106.518125  ...   100.731959   3.568631e+07
2016-12-31  113.273968   114.160635  ...   108.445124   3.201970e+07
2017-03-31  131.317097   132.165161  ...   126.532631   2.741482e+07
2017-06-30  147.961112   148.820000  ...   142.639105   2.716610e+07
2017-09-30  155.236350   156.260477  ...   150.277220   2.799135e+07
2017-12-31  166.961428   168.073175  ...   162.466309   2.597045e+07
2018-03-31  172.273606   174.097213  ...   168.018081   3.772625e+07
2018-06-30  181.206876   182.712500  ...   177.704693   2.835555e+07
2018-09-30  208.025556   209.894127  ...   204.819564   2.814258e+07
2018-12-31  203.907551   206.332041  ...   200.624250   4.042097e+07

[21 rows x 6 columns]
>>>
```

Other than finding the aggregated values for all columns of the dataset, it is possible for us to resample the data for a specific column. Let us create a bar plot that shows the yearly mean value for the Close attribute of our dataset. Just run the script given below:

```
plt.rcParams['figure.figsize'] = (7, 5)
data['Close'].resample('A').mean().plot(kind
='bar')
```

So that your whole script looks as follows:

```
import pandas as pd
import numpy as np

import matplotlib.pyplot as plt
import sys

sys.__stdout__ = sys.stdout
```

```
data = pd.read_csv(r'AAPL.csv')
data['Date'] =
data['Date'].apply(pd.to_datetime)
data.set_index('Date', inplace=True)
plt.rcParams['figure.figsize'] = (7, 5)
data['Close'].resample('A').mean().plot(kind
='bar')
plt.show()
```

The code should return the following plot:

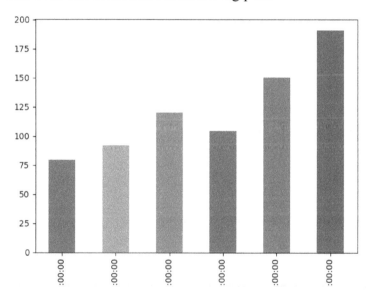

What we have done is that we simply called the *plot* function after the aggregate function then we passed to it the type of plot that we need to create.

Similarly, if you need to create a line plot that shows the monthly maximum stock price value for Close attribute, just run the script given below:

```
plt.rcParams['figure.figsize'] = (7, 5)
data['Close'].resample('M').max().plot(kind=
'line')
```

So that your whole code is as follows:

```python
import pandas as pd
import numpy as np

import matplotlib.pyplot as plt
import sys

sys.__stdout__ = sys.stdout

data = pd.read_csv(r'AAPL.csv')
data['Date'] = data['Date'].apply(pd.to_datetime)
data.set_index('Date', inplace=True)
plt.rcParams['figure.figsize'] = (7, 5)
data['Close'].resample('M').max().plot(kind='line')
plt.show()
```

The code will return the following plot:

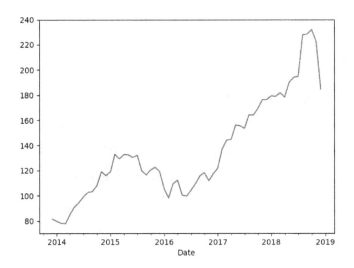

That is how powerful the Pandas library is. Since it is a popular library for use in performing data science tasks, you should learn to use it for creating various types of plots. In most cases, the library is used for importing, manipulating and cleaning datasets. However, as you have learned, it is a great tool for data visualization.

7-Data
Visualization with
Seaborn

The Seaborn library is based on the Matplotlib library and it helps in making data visualization easier. This library can be used for creating both categorical and distributional plots.

In this chapter, we will be using the titanic dataset. The Seaborn library comes loaded with this dataset, so your task is to call the *load_dataset* function then pass the name of this dataset to it as the parameter. The dataset will then be loaded into your workspace.

Let us import the necessary libraries, load the data and print its head:

```python
import pandas as pd
import numpy as np

import matplotlib.pyplot as plt
import seaborn as sns
import sys

sys.__stdout__ = sys.stdout

data = sns.load_dataset('titanic')

print(data.head())
```

The code prints the following:

```
     survived  pclass     sex   age  ...  deck  embark_town  alive  alone
0           0       3    male  22.0  ...   NaN  Southampton     no  False
1           1       1  female  38.0  ...     C    Cherbourg    yes  False
2           1       3  female  26.0  ...   NaN  Southampton    yes   True
3           1       1  female  35.0  ...     C  Southampton    yes  False
4           0       3    male  35.0  ...   NaN  Southampton     no   True

[5 rows x 15 columns]
>>>
```

The dataset comes with 15 rows and 891 rows showing the details of the passengers who were onboard the unfortunate titanic ship. We need to use the Seaborn library to extract various patterns from the dataset.

Distributional Plots

These are the types of plots that show how statistical data is distributed. We will be discussing the common distributional plots provided by the Seaborn library.

Dist Plot

We can call the *distplot()* function which shows the histogram distribution of a dataset for a column. To see the price distribution of the ticket for every passenger, we can run the following script:

```
sns.distplot(data['fare'])
```

So that your whole script is as follows:

```
import pandas as pd
import numpy as np

import matplotlib.pyplot as plt
```

```python
import seaborn as sns
import sys

sys.__stdout__ = sys.stdout

data = sns.load_dataset('titanic')

sns.distplot(data['fare'])
plt.show()
```

The script will return the following:

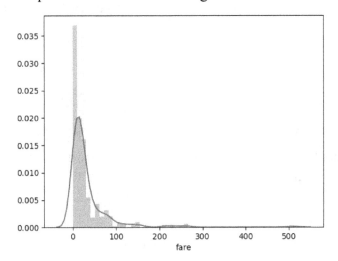

The above plot shows that most of the tickets have been sold between 0 and 50 dollars. The visible line shows the kernel density estimation. To remove the line, you can pass a value of *False* to the *kde* parameter. This is demonstrated below:

```python
sns.distplot(data['fare'], kde=False)
```

So that you have the following code:

```python
import pandas as pd
```

```
import numpy as np

import matplotlib.pyplot as plt
import seaborn as sns
import sys

sys.__stdout__ = sys.stdout

data = sns.load_dataset('titanic')

sns.distplot(data['fare'], kde=False)
plt.show()
```

The line will not be part of the output as shown below:

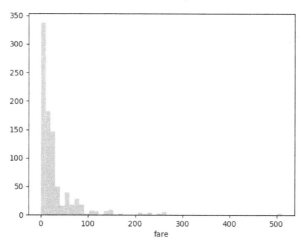

To specify the number of details that you need to see about the graph, use the *bins* parameter. The following script demonstrates this:

```
sns.distplot(data['fare'], kde=False,
bins=10)
```

The code should now be as follows:

```
import pandas as pd
```

```python
import numpy as np

import matplotlib.pyplot as plt
import seaborn as sns
import sys

sys.__stdout__ = sys.stdout

data = sns.load_dataset('titanic')

sns.distplot(data['fare'], kde=False, bins=10)

plt.show()
```

To return the following plot:

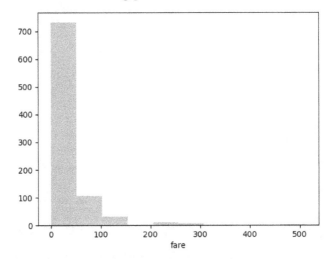

In the script, the number of bins was set to 10, hence, the data was distributed across 10 bins.

Joint Plot

We can use the *jointplot()* function to show the mutual

distribution of every column. Three parameters should be passed to the *jointplot()* function. The first parameter is the name of the column for which you need to show the distribution on the x-axis. The second parameter should be the name of the column for which you need to show the distribution on the y-axis. The third and final parameter should be the name of the data frame.

Let us now create a joint plot of the *age* and *fare* columns so that we may inspect any underlying relationship between the two. We only need to add the following script to our code:

```
sns.jointplot(x='age', y='fare', data=data)
```

So that we get the following data:

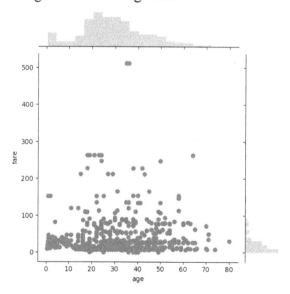

The above output clearly shows that a joint plot has three parts. At the top, we have the distribution plot for the column on the x-axis. On the right, we have the distribution plot for the column on the y-axis. In between, we have a scatter plot showing the mutual distribution of data across the columns. The output shown in the above plot shows that there exists no correlation between prices and fares.

If you need to create a different type of a joint plot, you only have to specify a value for the *kind* parameter. For example, instead of creating a scatter plot, we may need to show the distribution of the data using a hexagonal plot. To achieve this, we only have to pass the value *hex* to the *kind* parameter. The following script demonstrates this:

```python
sns.jointplot(x='age', y='fare', data=data,
kind='hex')
```

Your whole script should be as follows:

```python
import pandas as pd
import numpy as np

import matplotlib.pyplot as plt
import seaborn as sns
import sys

sys.__stdout__ = sys.stdout

data = sns.load_dataset('titanic')

sns.jointplot(x='age', y='fare', data=data,
kind='hex')

plt.show()
```

The generated plot should be as follows:

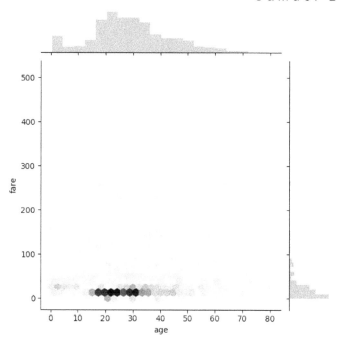

When creating a hexagon plot, the hexagon with the highest number of points will get a darker color. This means that from the above plot, most of the passengers are aged between 10 and 20 and most of the passengers paid between 10 and 50 for tickets.

Pair Plot

A pair plot is a type of distribution that creates a joint plot for all the possible combinations of the Boolean and numeric columns in the dataset. To generate one, you only have to call the *pairplot()* function and pass the name of the dataset to it as the parameter. The following script demonstrates this:

```
sns.pairplot(data)
```

The script may fail to run if the data has null values. That is why you should first remove all the null values from the dataset before you can execute the script. You can achieve this by running the following script:

```
data.dropna()
```

Now, make sure that your whole script is as follows:

```python
import pandas as pd
import numpy as np

import matplotlib.pyplot as plt
import seaborn as sns
import sys

sys.__stdout__ = sys.stdout

data = sns.load_dataset('titanic')
data2= data.dropna()


sns.pairplot(data2)
plt.show()
```

The code should return the following plot:

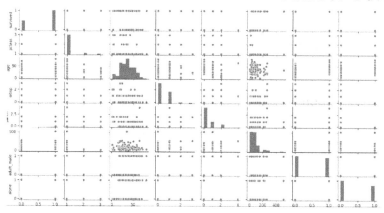

From the above pair plot, you can get the joint plots for all Boolean and numeric columns in our titanic dataset.

If there is a need for you to add information about the categorical column to the pair plot, you can use the *hue* parameter and pass the name of the categorical column to it as the argument. For example, the following script can help us to plot the gender information on the pair plot:

```
sns.pairplot(data2, hue='sex')
```

So that you have the following code:

```
import pandas as pd
import numpy as np

import matplotlib.pyplot as plt
import seaborn as sns
import sys

sys.__stdout__ = sys.stdout

data = sns.load_dataset('titanic')
data2= data.dropna()
```

```
sns.pairplot(data2, hue='sex')
plt.show()
```

Information for the male will be plotted in a different color from the information for females.

Rug Plot

This is a kind of plot that shows small bars along the x-axis for every point on the dataset. To create one, we only need to call the *rugplot()* function. The name of the column should be passed to the function. The following script can help us create a rug plot for the fare column of the Titanic dataset:

```
sns.rugplot(data['fare'])
```

For the whole script to be as follows:

```
import pandas as pd
import numpy as np

import matplotlib.pyplot as plt
import seaborn as sns
import sys

sys.__stdout__ = sys.stdout

data = sns.load_dataset('titanic')

sns.rugplot(data['fare'])
plt.show()
```

The script should return the following plot:

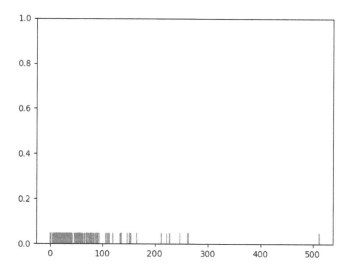

The above plot clearly that most of the fares are between 0 and 100, just as it was the case with the dist plot.

Categorical Plots

From the name, one can tell that categorical plots are used for plotting categorical data. In a categorical plot, the values are plotted in the categorical column against the other categorical column or numeric column. Let us discuss the most common categorical plots:

Bar Plot

A bar plot shows the mean value of every value in a categorical column against a numeric column. It is created by calling the *barplot()* function. The name of the categorical column should be the first argument to the function, the second column should be the numeric column while the third argument should be the name of the dataset.

For example, we can create a bar plot that shows the mean age of the male as well as female passengers. The following script can help us create the plot:

```
sns.barplot(x='sex', y='age', data=data)
```

The whole script should be as follows:

```
import pandas as pd
import numpy as np

import matplotlib.pyplot as plt
import seaborn as sns
import sys

sys.__stdout__ = sys.stdout

data = sns.load_dataset('titanic')

sns.barplot(x='sex', y='age', data=data)
plt.show()
```

The generated bar plot should be as follows:

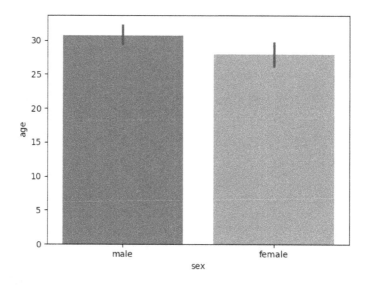

The plot clearly shows that the average age for all male passengers is above 30 while the average age of the female passengers is between 25 and 30.

Other than finding the average age, we can use a bar plot to calculate the other aggregate values for every category. This can be achieved by passing the aggregate function to the *estimator*. To get the standard deviation for the age of every gender, we can use the following script:

```python
import pandas as pd
import numpy as np

import matplotlib.pyplot as plt
import seaborn as sns
import sys

sys.__stdout__ = sys.stdout

data = sns.load_dataset('titanic')
```

```
sns.barplot(x='sex', y='age', data=data,
estimator=np.std)
plt.show()
```

The script will return the following bar plot:

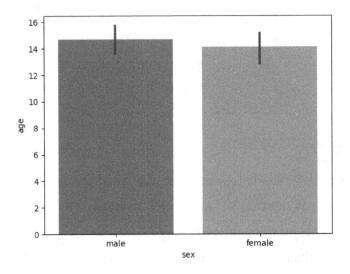

In the script, we have used the *std* aggregate function provided by the *numpy* library to compute the standard deviation of the ages of both the male and female passengers.

Count Plot

This type of plot is similar to the bar plot, with the difference being that it displays the count of categories in a specific column. A good application of this is when we need to calculate the total number or count of male and female passengers. We can use the following script for this:

```
sns.countplot(x='sex', data=data)
```

The whole script should be as follows:

```python
import pandas as pd
import numpy as np

import matplotlib.pyplot as plt
import seaborn as sns
import sys

sys.__stdout__ = sys.stdout

data = sns.load_dataset('titanic')

sns.countplot(x='sex', data=data)

plt.show()
```

The script should return the following plot:

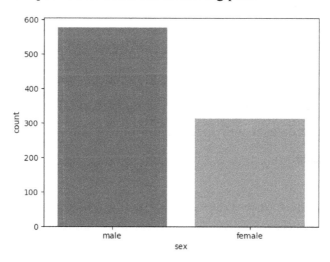

The output shows that males are more than females. There are about 300 females and close to 600 males.

Box Plot

For the case of categorical data, a box plot displays it in quartiles. The center or the line dividing the box into two shows the median of the data. The end of the box represents the upper quartile (75%) while the start of the box represents the lower quartile (25%). In some cases, the upper quartile is referred to as the 3rd quartile while the lower quartile is referred to as the 1st quartile. The part between the upper quartile and the lower quartile is known as the *Inter Quartile Range* (IQR) and helps in approximating 50% of the middle data.

The end of the upper whisker shows the maximum value in the data while the end of the lower whisker shows the minimum value in the data. Any points shown on the extremes represent the outliers in the data.

We want to create a box plot that shows the distribution of age for every gender. The first argument to the function should be the name of the categorical column (gender) while the second argument should be the name of the numerical column (age). The name of the dataset will then be the third parameter. Here is the script for this:

```
sns.boxplot(x='sex', y='age', data=data)
```

So the entire script will be:

```
import pandas as pd
import numpy as np

import matplotlib.pyplot as plt
import seaborn as sns
```

```
import sys

sys.__stdout__ = sys.stdout

data = sns.load_dataset('titanic')

sns.boxplot(x='sex', y='age', data=data)

plt.show()
```

The following plot should be returned:

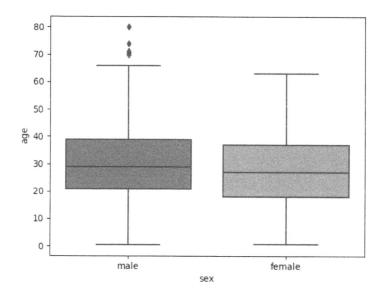

Let us analyze the box plot for the males. The first quartile starts at around 5 and ends at 22 which means that 25% of the passengers are aged between 5 and 22. The second quartile starts at around 23 and ends at around 28 which means that 25% of the passengers are aged between 23 and 28. Similarly, the third quartile starts and ends between 29 and 38, hence 25% passengers are aged within this range and finally the fourth or last quartile starts at 39 and ends around 76.

The dots above the upper whisker show that there are outliers, in that there are men whose ages don't lie within the quartiles.

To make your box plot more appealing, you can a layer of distribution to it. For example, if your goal is to see the box plots of forage of passengers both male and female, together with information showing whether they survived or not, use the *hue* parameter and pass the value of *survived* to it. The following script demonstrates this:

```
sns.boxplot(x='sex', y='age', data=data,
hue="survived")
```

The whole script should be as follows:

```
import pandas as pd
import numpy as np

import matplotlib.pyplot as plt
import seaborn as sns
import sys

sys.__stdout__ = sys.stdout

data = sns.load_dataset('titanic')

sns.boxplot(x='sex', y='age', data=data,
hue="survived")

plt.show()
```

The generated plot should be as follows:

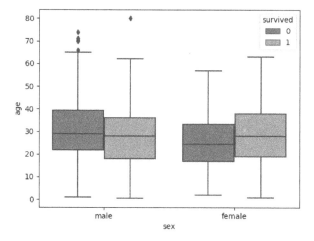

Other than the information about the age of the passengers, the above plot also shows the distribution of passengers who survived. The plot shows that most young males survived compared to females.

V i o l i n   P l o t

This type of plot is the same as the box plot, but with a violin plot, we can display all components corresponding to a data point. To create a violin plot, we call the *violinplot()* function. The first parameter to the function is the name of the categorical column, the second parameter is the name of the numeric column while the third column is the name of the dataset.

Let us create a violin plot that shows the distribution of age against every gender. Here is the script:

```
sns.violinplot(x='sex', y='age', data=data)
```

So that the whole script is as follows:

```python
import pandas as pd
import numpy as np

import matplotlib.pyplot as plt
import seaborn as sns
import sys

sys.__stdout__ = sys.stdout

data = sns.load_dataset('titanic')

sns.violinplot(x='sex', y='age', data=data)

plt.show()
```

The script should return the following plot upon execution:

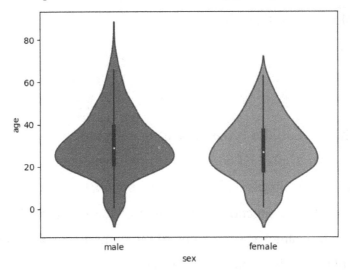

From the above plot, it is very clear that a violin plot can provide more information about the underlying data compared to a box plot. Instead of plotting the quartiles only, the violin plot shows us all components that correspond to the data. The area within the violin that is shown to be thicker means that it has a higher number of instances for the age. For the case of the violin plot for the male, it is clear that most males are aged between 20 and 40.

You can use the *hue* parameter to add another categorical variable to the violin, just in the same way we did with box plots. The following script can be used for this:

```
sns.violinplot(x='sex', y='age', data=data,
hue='survived')
```

It should be added to the script as follows:

```
import pandas as pd
import numpy as np

import matplotlib.pyplot as plt
import seaborn as sns
import sys

sys.__stdout__ = sys.stdout

data = sns.load_dataset('titanic')

sns.violinplot(x='sex', y='age', data=data,
hue='survived')

plt.show()
```

The code should generate the following plot:

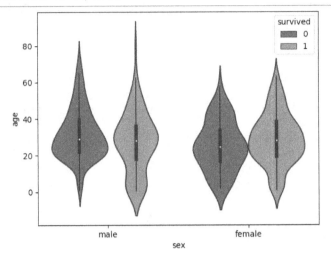

The above violin plot has more information than the previous one. For example, a comparison between the bottoms of the violin for males who survived with the violin for males who did not survive shows that the former is thicker than the latter. This tells us that the number of young males who survived is more than the number of young males who did not survive. It is true that a violin plot will show much information compared to a box plot, but much time is required to be able to interpret it.

Instead of creating two different graphs showing passengers who survived and those who did not survive, you can create one violin plot divided into two halves, with one representing the survivors and the other half representing the non-survivors. To do so, call the *violinplot()* function and pass a value of *True* to the *split* parameter. This is demonstrated below:

```
sns.violinplot(x='sex', y='age', data=data,
hue='survived', split=True)
```

So that the whole script is as follows:

```python
import pandas as pd
import numpy as np

import matplotlib.pyplot as plt
import seaborn as sns
import sys

sys.__stdout__ = sys.stdout

data = sns.load_dataset('titanic')

sns.violinplot(x='sex', y='age', data=data,
hue='survived', split=True)
plt.show()
```

The script should return the following plot:

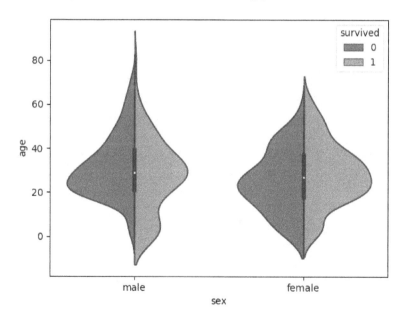

From the above plot, you can easily make a comparison between both males and females who survived and those who did not survive.

Box plots and violin plots are very useful. However, if your target audience is non-technical, it will be good for you to use a box plot since it is easy to interpret. However, if your data presentation targets researchers, it will be more convenient for you to use a violin plot since it will occupy less space and you will be able to convey much information within a short period of time.

Strip Plot

The strip plot helps us create a scatter plot in which one of the variables is categorical. In the pair plot and joint plot, we had to scatter plots in which the two variables where numeric. The strip plot is different in that one of the variables is categorical, and for every category of the categorical variable, a scatter plot will be shown with respect to the numeric column.

To create a strip plot, we call the *stripplot()* function. The first parameter to the function is the name of the categorical variable, the second parameter is the name of the numeric variable while the third variable is the name of the dataset. Consider the script given below:

```
sns.stripplot(x='sex', y='age', data=data)
```

Here is the whole script:

```
import pandas as pd
import numpy as np

import matplotlib.pyplot as plt
```

```
import seaborn as sns
import sys

sys.__stdout__ = sys.stdout

data = sns.load_dataset('titanic')

sns.stripplot(x='sex', y='age', data=data)

plt.show()
```

The following plot should be generated:

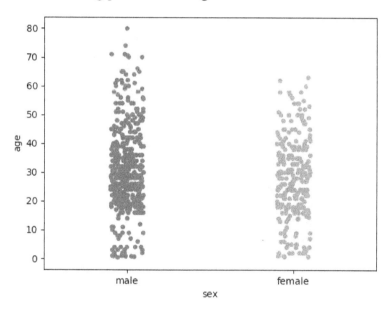

The scattered plots for the ages of both males and females have been plotted. The data points have been plotted in the form of strips. The comprehension of data distribution in such a form is difficult. To be able to comprehend, use the *jitter* parameter and set its value to *True*. This will add some noise to the data. The following script demonstrates this:

```
sns.stripplot(x='sex', y='age', data=data,
jitter=True)
```

For the whole script to be as follows:

```
import pandas as pd
import numpy as np

import matplotlib.pyplot as plt
import seaborn as sns
import sys

sys.__stdout__ = sys.stdout

data = sns.load_dataset('titanic')

sns.stripplot(x='sex', y='age', data=data,
jitter=True)
plt.show()
```

You will then be able to get a clear view regarding the data distribution about the genders.

Just like a violin plot, it is possible for us to add an additional categorical column to a strip plot by use of the *hue* parameter. This is demonstrated below:

```
sns.stripplot(x='sex', y='age', data=data,
jitter=True, hue='survived')
```

For the whole script to be as follows:

```
import pandas as pd
import numpy as np

import matplotlib.pyplot as plt
import seaborn as sns
```

```
import sys

sys.__stdout__ = sys.stdout

data = sns.load_dataset('titanic')

sns.stripplot(x='sex', y='age', data=data,
jitter=True, hue='survived')
plt.show()
```

The plot should now be as follows:

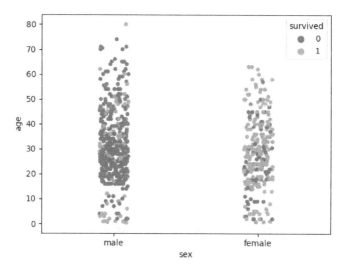

The plot clearly shows that there are many young women who survived than those who did not survive.

To have a more clear view of data, we can split the strip plot in the same way we did for the violin plot. This can be done as follows:

```
sns.stripplot(x='sex', y='age', data=data,
jitter=True, hue='survived', split=True)
```

For the whole script to be as follows:

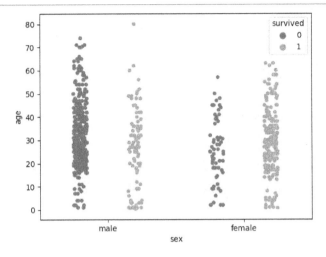

It is now easy for you to see the distribution of age between the males and females who survived and those who did not survive.

S w a r m   P l o t

This type of plot is a combination of a strip plot and a violin plot. In this type of plot, the points are adjusted in such a way that they don't overlap. To demonstrate this, we will create a swarm plot that shows the distribution of age against gender. We will do this by calling the *swarmplot()* function. The first parameter to the function should be the name of the categorical column, the second parameter should be the name of the numerical column while the third parameter should be the name of the dataset. The following script demonstrates this:

```
sns.swarmplot(x='sex', y='age', data=data)
```

For the whole script to be as follows:

```python
import pandas as pd
import numpy as np

import matplotlib.pyplot as plt
import seaborn as sns
import sys

sys.__stdout__ = sys.stdout

data = sns.load_dataset('titanic')

sns.swarmplot(x='sex', y='age', data=data)
plt.show()
```

The plot should be generated from the script:

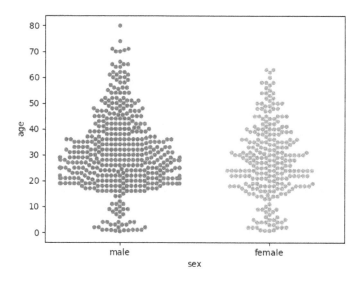

The data points are scattered just as it was the case with a strip plot, but there is a difference in that the points don't overlap. Instead of that, they have been arranged well to give a clear view similar to what we had with a violin plot.

We can also use the *hue* parameter to add another categorical column to our swarm plot. The following script demonstrates this:

```
sns.swarmplot(x='sex', y='age', data=data,
hue='survived')
```

For the whole script to be as follows:

```
import pandas as pd
import numpy as np

import matplotlib.pyplot as plt
import seaborn as sns
import sys

sys.__stdout__ = sys.stdout

data = sns.load_dataset('titanic')

sns.swarmplot(x='sex', y='age', data=data,
hue='survived')
plt.show()
```

The following swarm plot should be generated:

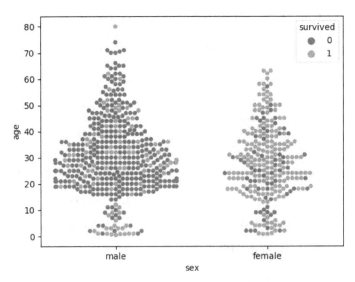

The output shows that few men survived compared to women.

The reason is that for the case of the male plot, we have many blue points (passengers who did not survive) and few orange dots (passengers who survived). We can also tell that many numbers of women survived compared to those who did not survive. This is because the number of orange dots (passengers who survived) is many than the blue dots (passengers who did not survive).

It is also possible for us to split the swarm plot just as we did with the box and violin plots. The following script explains how we can do it:

```python
sns.swarmplot(x='sex', y='age', data=data,
hue='survived', split=True)
```

For the whole script to be as follows:

```python
import pandas as pd
import numpy as np

import matplotlib.pyplot as plt
import seaborn as sns
import sys

sys.__stdout__ = sys.stdout

data = sns.load_dataset('titanic')

sns.swarmplot(x='sex', y='age', data=data,
hue='survived', split=True)
plt.show()
```

The script will return the following plot:

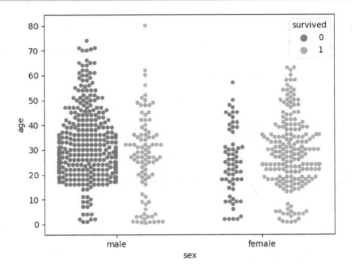

The plot clearly shows that there us a high number of women who survived compared to men.

Combined Violin and Swarm Plots

Swarm plots are not suitable for use in large datasets. The reason is that since each point has to be plotted, they will not scale well. For individuals who like to use a swarm plot, they can get a better outcome if they combine two plots. For example, we can combine a violin and swarm plot using the script given below:

```
sns.violinplot(x='sex', y='age', data=data)
sns.swarmplot(x='sex', y='age', data=data,
color='black')
```

So that we get the following as the whole script:

```python
import pandas as pd
import numpy as np

import matplotlib.pyplot as plt
import seaborn as sns
import sys

sys.__stdout__ = sys.stdout

data = sns.load_dataset('titanic')

sns.violinplot(x='sex', y='age', data=data)
sns.swarmplot(x='sex', y='age', data=data,
color='black')
plt.show()
```

The code will generate the following plot:

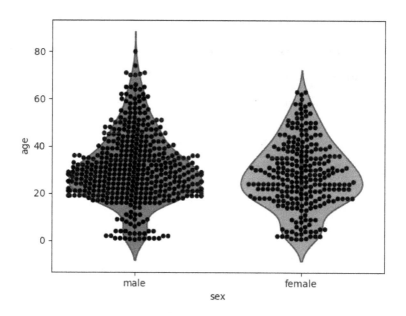

There you have it! The two plots combined to give a clear picture of how the data is distributed.

From all the plots we have created with Seaborn, you can tell
that it is an advanced visualization library. Most of the plots we
have plotted in this chapter are advanced.

Matrix Plots

Other than the distributional and categorical plots, we can use
the Seaborn library to create other types of plots. The Seaborn
library is good for the creation of Matrix plots.

A matrix plot shows data in the form of rows and columns. Let
is discuss the various types of matrix plots that we can plot with
the Seaborn library:

Heat maps

The purpose of heat maps is to show the correlation between
numeric columns using a matrix. Note that for you to be in a
position to draw a heat map, you must have a good understanding
of both rows and columns.

We will continue to use the Titanic dataset. Let us print the
first five rows of the dataset:


```python
import numpy as np
import pandas as pd

import matplotlib.pyplot as plt
import seaborn as sns
import sys

sys.__stdout__ = sys.stdout

data = sns.load_dataset('titanic')
```

```
print(data.head())
```

The code will return the following:

```
   survived  pclass     sex   age  ...  deck  embark_town  alive  alone
0         0       3    male  22.0  ...   NaN  Southampton     no  False
1         1       1  female  38.0  ...     C    Cherbourg    yes  False
2         1       3  female  26.0  ...   NaN  Southampton    yes   True
3         1       1  female  35.0  ...     C  Southampton    yes  False
4         0       3    male  35.0  ...   NaN  Southampton     no   True

[5 rows x 15 columns]
```

The headers for the columns contain very useful information as shown above. The row headers are only made up of indices. For us to be able to create the matrix plots, we need to have useful information for both the rows and column headers. We can achieve this by calling the *corr()* function. When we call the *corr()* function on the dataset, it will return the correlations that exist between the numeric columns contained in the dataset. Here is how to invoke the function on the dataset:

```
data.corr()
```

So you can have the following script:

```
import numpy as np
import pandas as pd

import matplotlib.pyplot as plt
import seaborn as sns
import sys

sys.__stdout__ = sys.stdout

data = sns.load_dataset('titanic')

print(data.corr())
```

This should return the following output:

```
            survived     pclass    ...    adult_male     alone
survived    1.000000  -0.338481    ...     -0.557080  -0.203367
pclass     -0.338481   1.000000    ...      0.094035   0.135207
age        -0.077221  -0.369226    ...      0.280328   0.198270
sibsp      -0.035322   0.083081    ...     -0.253586  -0.584471
parch       0.081629   0.018443    ...     -0.349943  -0.583398
fare        0.257307  -0.549500    ...     -0.182024  -0.271832
adult_male -0.557080   0.094035    ...      1.000000   0.404744
alone      -0.203367   0.135207    ...      0.404744   1.000000

[8 rows x 8 columns]
```

The above output shows that both the rows and columns give very useful header information. We can use these correlation values to create a heat map. To do this, we only have to call the *heatmap()* function then we pass the correlation dataframe to it as the argument. The following script demonstrates this:

```
corr = dataset.corr()
sns.heatmap(corr)
```

You should now have the following script:

```
import numpy as np
import pandas as pd

import matplotlib.pyplot as plt
import seaborn as sns
import sys

sys.__stdout__ = sys.stdout

data = sns.load_dataset('titanic')

corr = data.corr()
sns.heatmap(corr)
plt.show()
```

The code will generate the following:

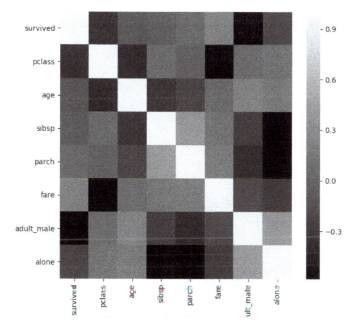

The above plot shows that a heat map creates a box for every combination of rows and a column. The color of every box is determined by the gradient. If a high correlation exists between two features, the resulting box or cell is white. Consequently, if there is no correlation exists between the two features, the resulting cell or box will be black.

It is possible for us to show the correlation values on the plot. To achieve this, we use the *annot* parameter and set its value to *True*. This is demonstrated below:

```
corr = data.corr()
sns.heatmap(corr, annot=True)
```

So that you end up with the following script:

```python
import numpy as np
import pandas as pd

import matplotlib.pyplot as plt
import seaborn as sns
import sys

sys.__stdout__ = sys.stdout

data = sns.load_dataset('titanic')

corr = data.corr()
sns.heatmap(corr, annot=True)
plt.show()
```

The script will return the following plot:

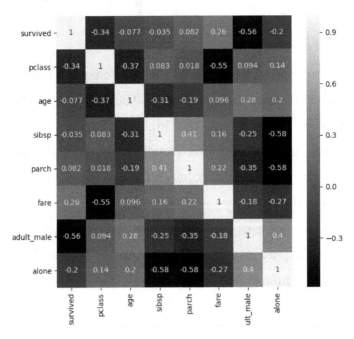

The correlation values have been added. If you need to change the color of the heat map, you can use the *cmap* parameter and pass a value to it. The following script demonstrates this:

```
corr = data.corr()
sns.heatmap(corr, cmap='winter')
```

The whole script should be as follows:

```
import numpy as np
import pandas as pd

import matplotlib.pyplot as plt
import seaborn as sns
import sys

sys.__stdout__ = sys.stdout

data = sns.load_dataset('titanic')

corr = data.corr()
sns.heatmap(corr, cmap='winter')
plt.show()
```

The following should be the generated plot:

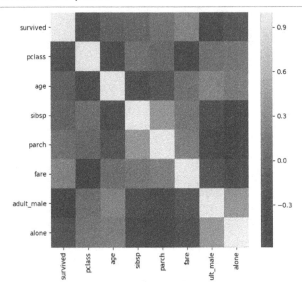

Instead of creating a correlation between all the columns, we can call the *pivot_table* function and specify the index, column and the values that we need to see in correspondence to the index and columns.

We now want to see how the *pivot_table* function works. Instead of the titanic dataset, we will now use the *Flights* dataset. This dataset has details of passengers who travelled in every month. We can load and see the first few rows of the dataset by running the following script:

```python
import numpy as np
import pandas as pd

import matplotlib.pyplot as plt
import seaborn as sns
import sys

sys.__stdout__ = sys.stdout
```

```
data = sns.load_dataset('flights')
print(data.head())
```

The script will return the first 5 rows of the dataset as shown below:

```
     year       month  passengers
0    1949     January         112
1    1949    February         118
2    1949       March         132
3    1949       April         129
4    1949         May         121
```

We can now call the *pivot_table* function and generate a heat map that shows the number of passengers that travelled in a particular month of a particular year. This means that the value of the *index* parameter will be the *month*. This parameter represents the rows. We will also use the *column* parameter and give it the value *year*. The value of the *values* parameter will be set to *passengers*. This is shown below:

```
data2 = data.pivot_table(index='month',
columns='year', values='passengers')
sns.heatmap(data2)
```

You should have the following script:

You should get the following plot:

```
import numpy as np
import pandas as pd

import matplotlib.pyplot as plt
```

```python
import seaborn as sns
import sys

sys.__stdout__ = sys.stdout

data = sns.load_dataset('flights')

data2 = data.pivot_table(index='month',
columns='year', values='passengers')
sns.heatmap(data2)
plt.show()
```

The plot shows that there were few number of passengers in the first years. As the years progressed, the number of passengers increased.

With the above plot, some of the cells or boxes are overlapping and in some instances, it is difficult for us to identify the boundaries between various cells. To make these boundary lines become clearer, we can use the *linecolor* and *linewidth* parameters. This is demonstrated below:

```
data2 = data.pivot_table(index='month',
columns='year', values='passengers' )
sns.heatmap(data2, linecolor='blue',
linewidth=1)
```

So you should have the following script:

```
import numpy as np
import pandas as pd

import matplotlib.pyplot as plt
import seaborn as sns
import sys

sys.__stdout__ = sys.stdout

data = sns.load_dataset('flights')

data2 = data.pivot_table(index='month',
columns='year', values='passengers' )
sns.heatmap(data2, linecolor='blue',
linewidth=1)
plt.show()
```

You should get the following plot:

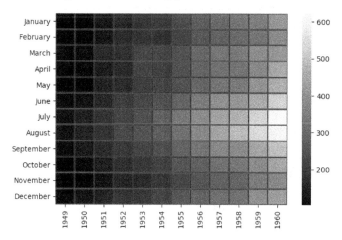

We used a value of *blue* for the *linecolor* parameter and a value of 1 for the *linewidth* parameter. That is why the boundary lines have been printed in blue color.

If you need to have thicker boundaries, just increase the value of the parameter *linewidth*.

Cluster Map

This is another type of matrix plot that we can create with the Seaborn library. A cluster map uses hierarchical clustering so as to cluster the rows and columns of a matrix.

To demonstrate how to create one, we will plot a cluster map that shows the number of passengers who travelled in a particular month and in a particular year. We will do this using the *clustermap()* function as shown below:

```
data2 = data.pivot_table(index='month',
columns='year', values='passengers')
sns.clustermap(data2)
```

You should have the following script:

```
import numpy as np
import pandas as pd

import matplotlib.pyplot as plt
import seaborn as sns
import sys

sys.__stdout__ = sys.stdout

data = sns.load_dataset('flights')
```

```
data2 = data.pivot_table(index='month',
columns='year', values='passengers')
sns.clustermap(data2)
plt.show()
```

The script should return the following result:

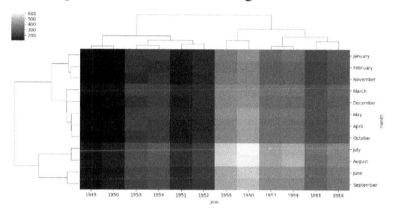

When creating a cluster map, we have to call the *clustermap()* function as we have done above and pass to it meaning headers for rows and columns. The output shows that the months and years were clustered together depending on the number of passengers that travelled on a particular month.

Seaborn Grids

In Seaborn, grids allow us to modify the subplots based on the features that have been used in the plots. Let us discuss these:

Pair grids

You already know what a pair plot is as we discussed it under distributional plots. It can be used to show the various combinations of the numeric columns of a dataset.

Let us have a review of the pair plot before moving to the pair grid. We will use the iris dataset which comes with the Seaborn library. The dataset shows the sepal and petal measurements of various flow species. The following script can help us to load the dataset:

```python
import numpy as np
import pandas as pd

import seaborn as sns
import matplotlib.pyplot as plt
import sys

sys.__stdout__ = sys.stdout

data = sns.load_dataset('iris')
print(data.head())
```

The script will return the following:

```
   sepal_length  sepal_width  petal_length  petal_width  species
0           5.1          3.5           1.4          0.2  setosa
1           4.9          3.0           1.4          0.2  setosa
2           4.7          3.2           1.3          0.2  setosa
3           4.6          3.1           1.5          0.2  setosa
4           5.0          3.6           1.4          0.2  setosa
```

Those are the first 5 rows of the dataset. The data shows the width and length of sepals and petals of the various flower species. We can create a pair plot for this dataset. We only have to invoke the *pairplot()* function as shown below:

```python
import numpy as np
import pandas as pd

import seaborn as sns
import matplotlib.pyplot as plt
```

```
import sys

sys.__stdout__ = sys.stdout

data = sns.load_dataset('iris')

sns.pairplot(data)
plt.show()
```

You should get something similar to the following:

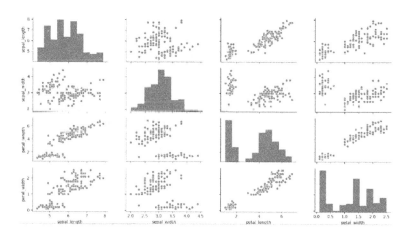

Now that we have a pair plot, we can plot a pair grid and see what makes the two different. The process of creating a pair grid is simple as we are only required to pass the name of the dataset to the *PairGrid* function as shown below:

```
sns.PairGrid(data)
```

Your script should be as follows:

```
import numpy as np
import pandas as pd
```

```
import seaborn as sns
import matplotlib.pyplot as plt
import sys

sys.__stdout__ = sys.stdout

data = sns.load_dataset('iris')

sns.PairGrid(data)
plt.show()
```

The code should return the following plot:

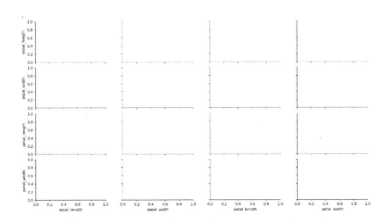

The output shows empty grids. That is how the pair grid function works. It generates an empty set of grids representing all the features contained in the dataset.

We can now call the *map* function on the object that has been returned by the pair grid function then we pass to it the type of the plot that we need to generate on the grids. Let us use a pair grid to plot a scatter plot:

```
grids = sns.PairGrid(data)
grids.map(plt.scatter)
```

So that the whole script is as follows:

```python
import numpy as np
import pandas as pd

import seaborn as sns
import matplotlib.pyplot as plt
import sys

sys.__stdout__ = sys.stdout

data = sns.load_dataset('iris')

grids = sns.PairGrid(data)
grids.map(plt.scatter)
plt.show()
```

The script should return the following plot:

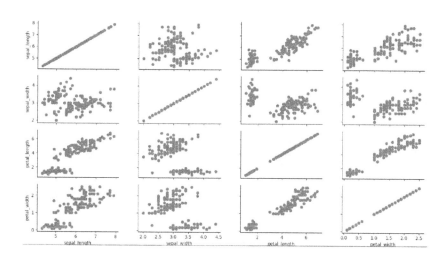

There are the scatter plots showing all combinations of numeric columns in the dataset.

It is possible for you to create different types of graphs on the plot. You can for example plot a distribution plot on the diagonal, a scatter plot on the lower part of the diagonal and a kdeplot on the upper half of the diagonal.

You only need to use map_diagonal, map_lower and map_upper functions, respectively. The parameter to the functions should be the type of plot that is to be drawn as shown below:

```
grids = sns.PairGrid(data)
grids.map_diag(sns.distplot)
grids.map_upper(sns.kdeplot)
grids.map_lower(plt.scatter)
```

You should now have the following script:

```
import numpy as np
import pandas as pd

import seaborn as sns
import matplotlib.pyplot as plt
import sys

sys.__stdout__ = sys.stdout

data = sns.load_dataset('iris')

grids = sns.PairGrid(data)
grids = sns.PairGrid(data)
grids.map_diag(sns.distplot)
grids.map_upper(sns.kdeplot)
grids.map_lower(plt.scatter)
plt.show()
```

The script should return the following plot:

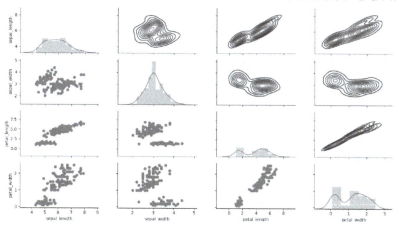

From the above image, you can tell that the power grid is a powerful function. The distributional plots have been plotted on the diagonals, the kernel density plots have been plotted on the upper half while the scatter plots have been plotted on the lower half.

Facet Grids

We use facet grids to plot two or more categorical features against two or more numeric features. We will create a facet grid that shows the distribution plot of gender vs. alive with respect to the passengers' age. We will use the titanic dataset for this.

To load the dataset, run the following script:

```python
import numpy as np
import pandas as pd

import matplotlib.pyplot as plt
import seaborn as sns
import sys

sys.__stdout__ = sys.stdout
```

```
data = sns.load_dataset('titanic')
```

You can check the first 5 rows of the dataset using the *head()* function as shown below:

```python
import numpy as np
import pandas as pd

import matplotlib.pyplot as plt
import seaborn as sns
import sys

sys.__stdout__ = sys.stdout

data = sns.load_dataset('titanic')
print(data.head())
```

It should return the following:

```
   survived  pclass     sex   age  ...  deck  embark_town  alive  alone
0         0       3    male  22.0  ...   NaN  Southampton     no  False
1         1       1  female  38.0  ...     C    Cherbourg    yes  False
2         1       3  female  26.0  ...   NaN  Southampton    yes   True
3         1       1  female  35.0  ...     C  Southampton    yes  False
4         0       3    male  35.0  ...   NaN  Southampton     no   True

[5 rows x 15 columns]
```

To create a facet grid, we use the *FacetGrid()* function. You should pass the name of the dataset as the first parameter to the function, the second parameter as the feature to be plotted on the columns using *col* parameter, and finally the feature to be plotted on the rows using the *row* parameter. The function will return an object. If you need to state the type of plot you need to create, use the *map* function as we did with the pair grid function. Here is how to use the *FaceGrid()* function:

```
grid = sns.FacetGrid(data=data, col='alive',
row='sex')
grid.map(sns.distplot, 'age')
```

So you should have the following script:

```
import numpy as np
import pandas as pd

import matplotlib.pyplot as plt
import seaborn as sns
import sys

sys.__stdout__ = sys.stdout

data = sns.load_dataset('titanic')
grid = sns.FacetGrid(data=data, col='alive',
row='sex')
grid.map(sns.distplot, 'age')
plt.show()
```

You should get the following plot upon executing the code:

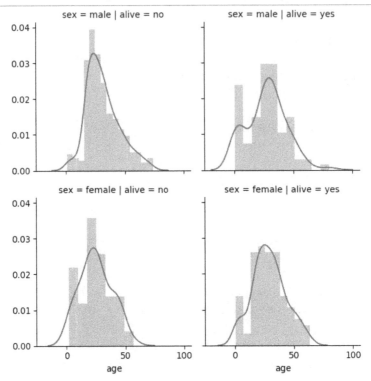

The above output shows that we have four plots. Each plot shows a combination of gender and the survival of the passenger. The columns show information about the survival while the rows show information about sex since that what we specified in the *FacetGrid()* function.

The first row and the first column show the age distribution in which the sex is male and the passengers did not survive. The first row and the second column show the age distribution of the passengers whose sex is male and survived. The second row and first column show the age distribution of passengers whose age is female and did not survive. The second row and second column show the age distribution of the passengers whose sex is female and survived.

Other than creating distribution plots of one feature, it is possible for us to create scatter plots with two features on the facet grid.

Here is a script that plots a scatter plot for the age and fare for both genders of passengers who survived as well as those who did not survive:

```
grid = sns.FacetGrid(data= data, col=
'alive', row = 'sex')
grid.map(plt.scatter, 'age', 'fare')
```

You should now have the following script:

```
import numpy as np
import pandas as pd

import matplotlib.pyplot as plt
import seaborn as sns
import sys

sys.__stdout__ = sys.stdout

data = sns.load_dataset('titanic')
grid = sns.FacetGrid(data= data, col=
'alive', row = 'sex')
grid.map(plt.scatter, 'age', 'fare')
plt.show()
```

The following plot should be generated:

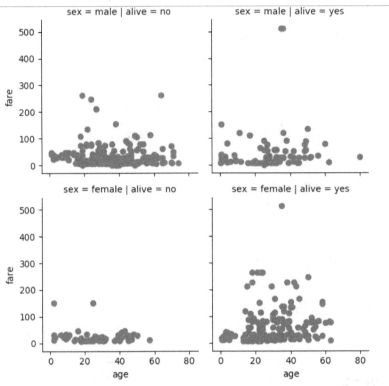

Regression Plots

Regression plots are used for performing regression analysis on either two or more variables. We will be creating a linear model plot that plots the linear relationship between two variables together with the best-fit regression line depending on the data. We will use the *diamond* dataset that comes with the Seaborn library. The following code can help you to load the dataset:

```python
import numpy as np
import pandas as pd

import matplotlib.pyplot as plt
```

```
import seaborn as sns
import sys

sys.__stdout__ = sys.stdout

data = sns.load_dataset('diamonds')
```

To see the first 5 rows of the dataset, invoke the *head()* function as shown below:

```
import numpy as np
import pandas as pd

import matplotlib.pyplot as plt
import seaborn as sns
import sys

sys.__stdout__ = sys.stdout

data = sns.load_dataset('diamonds')
print(data.head())
```

The dataset looks as shown below:

```
   carat     cut color clarity depth table price    x     y     z
0   0.23   Ideal     E     SI2  61.5  55.0   326  3.95  3.98  2.43
1   0.21 Premium     E     SI1  59.8  61.0   326  3.89  3.84  2.31
2   0.23    Good     E     VS1  56.9  65.0   327  4.05  4.07  2.31
3   0.29 Premium     I     VS2  62.4  58.0   334  4.20  4.23  2.63
4   0.31    Good     J     SI2  63.3  58.0   335  4.34  4.35  2.75
```

The dataset simply shows the various features of diamond including depth, weight, price, etc.

We need to create a plot that shows the linear relationship between the carat and the price of the diamond. The weight and price of the diamond are directly proportional, meaning that a heavier diamond will have a higher price. We need to check

whether this is true depending on the information that we get from
the dataset.

A linear model can be created by calling the *lmplot()* function.
The first parameter to the function should be the name of the
feature that you need to plot on the x-axis, the second parameter
should be the feature that you need to plot on the y-axis while the
third and the last parameter should be the name of the dataset as
demonstrated below:

```
sns.lmplot(x='carat', y='price', data=data)
```

This means that you should have the following script:

```
import numpy as np
import pandas as pd

import matplotlib.pyplot as plt
import seaborn as sns
import sys

sys.__stdout__ = sys.stdout

data = sns.load_dataset('diamonds')

sns.lmplot(x='carat', y='price', data=data)
plt.show()
```

The script should return the following plot:

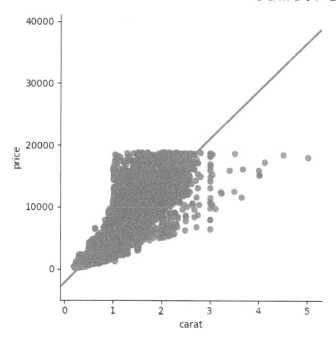

The output shows that the two have a linear relationship.

It is possible for us to plot multiple linear models that are based on a categorical feature. The name of the feature should be used as the value of the *hue* parameter. A good example is when you need to have multiple linear models showing the relationship between the carat and the price of the diamond depending on the cut of the diamond. In such a case, the *lmplot()* function can be used as shown below:

```
sns.lmplot(x='carat', y='price', data=data,
hue='cut')
```

Your script should be as follows:

```
import numpy as np
import pandas as pd
```

```python
import matplotlib.pyplot as plt
import seaborn as sns
import sys

sys.__stdout__ = sys.stdout

data = sns.load_dataset('diamonds')

sns.lmplot(x='carat', y='price', data=data,
hue='cut')
plt.show()
```

To return the plot given below:

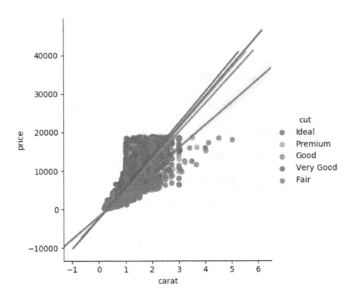

The plot shows that the linear relationship between the two, that is, the carat and the price of the diamond is steepest for an ideal cut diamond, which is what we expected, and this relationship is shallowest for the fair cut diamond.

Other than plotting the data for the cut feature using different hues, it is possible for us to plot one plot for every cut. We can achieve this using the *cols* attribute and passing the name of the column to it. This is demonstrated below:

```python
sns.lmplot(x='carat', y='price', data=data,
col='cut')
```

Here is the complete script:

```python
import numpy as np
import pandas as pd

import matplotlib.pyplot as plt
import seaborn as sns
import sys

sys.__stdout__ = sys.stdout

data = sns.load_dataset('diamonds')

sns.lmplot(x='carat', y='price', data=data,
col='cut')
plt.show()
```

The script should return the following plot:

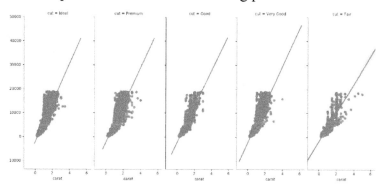

The output shows that there is a separate column for every

value in the cut column fo our dataset.

The size and the aspect ratio of the plots are changeable by use of the *size* and *aspect* parameters respectively. The following script demonstrates how to use these:

```
sns.lmplot(x='carat', y = 'price', data=
data, col = 'cut', aspect = 0.6, size = 9 )
```

The complete code should be as shown below:

```
import numpy as np
import pandas as pd

import matplotlib.pyplot as plt
import seaborn as sns
import sys

sys.__stdout__ = sys.stdout

data = sns.load_dataset('diamonds')

sns.lmplot(x='carat', y = 'price', data=
data, col = 'cut', aspect = 0.6, size = 9 )
plt.show()
```

You will find that the size and the aspect ratio of the plots have improved. The purpose of the *aspect* parameter is to define the aspect ratio between the width and the height. Since we have used an aspect value of 0.6, it means that the width will be 0.6 of the height. This is very clear in the output.

You should notice that it is true that the size of the plot has changed, but the size of the font is still small. Let us discuss how to change the size and styles used in plots using the Seaborn library.

Styling Plots

With the Seaborn library, we have access to various ways to style our plots. Let us discuss some of these:

Set style

Whenever you need to set the style of the grid, call the *set_style()* function. Some of the parameters accepted by this function include whitegrid, dark, darkgrid, white and ticks. Let us use the Titanic dataset to demonstrate how to use these.

First, load the dataset by running the following script:

```python
import numpy as np
import pandas as pd

import matplotlib.pyplot as plt
import seaborn as sns
import sys

sys.__stdout__ = sys.stdout
data = sns.load_dataset('titanic')
```

Here is the script for creating a dark grid plot:

```python
sns.set_style('darkgrid')
sns.distplot(data['fare'])
```

So you should have the following as the complete code:

```python
import numpy as np
import pandas as pd

import matplotlib.pyplot as plt
import seaborn as sns
import sys
```

```
sys.__stdout__ = sys.stdout

data = sns.load_dataset('titanic')

sns.set_style('darkgrid')
sns.distplot(data['fare'])
plt.show()
```

The script should return the following plot:

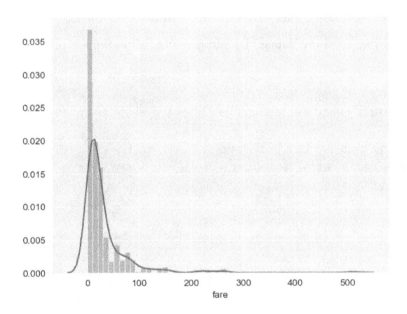

The output shows that the background is dark and with grids.
Let us now see how the *whitegrid* parameter works:

```
import numpy as np
import pandas as pd

import matplotlib.pyplot as plt
import seaborn as sns
import sys
```

```
sys.__stdout__ = sys.stdout

data = sns.load_dataset('titanic')

sns.set_style('whitegrid')
sns.distplot(data['fare'])
plt.show()
```

The code will return the following plot:

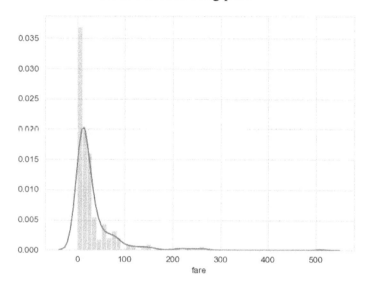

The output shows that we still have our grids but the background is no longer dark grey. The *dark* parameter will work as follows:

```
import numpy as np
import pandas as pd

import matplotlib.pyplot as plt
import seaborn as sns
import sys

sys.__stdout__ = sys.stdout
```

```python
data = sns.load_dataset('titanic')

sns.set_style('dark')
sns.distplot(data['fare'])
plt.show()
```

It should generate the following plot:

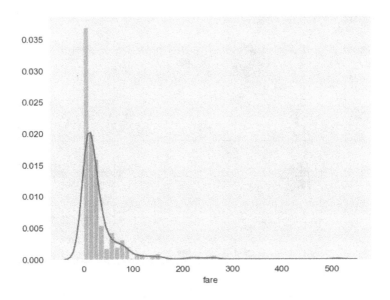

The grids are no longer visible. This is because we used the *dark* parameter without the grids. It created a dark background without the grids. This is how the *white* parameter works:

```python
import numpy as np
import pandas as pd

import matplotlib.pyplot as plt
import seaborn as sns
import sys
```

```
sys.__stdout__ = sys.stdout

data = sns.load_dataset('titanic')

sns.set_style('white')
sns.distplot(data['fare'])
plt.show()
```

The script will generate the following plot:

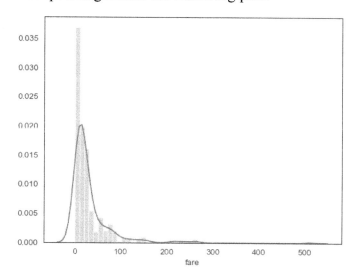

The background is now white and without grid. This is because we have used the *white* parameter without *grids*.

Seaborn was developed on top of Matplotlib, meaning that you can always use the pyplot module to change the size of the plot. This is demonstrated below:

```
import numpy as np
import pandas as pd

import matplotlib.pyplot as plt
import seaborn as sns
```

```
import sys

sys.__stdout__ = sys.stdout

data = sns.load_dataset('titanic')

plt.figure(figsize=(9,5))
sns.distplot(data['fare'])
plt.show()
```

What we have done is that we have set the height and the width of the plot to 9 and 5 inches respectively. You will notice that the generated plot will be a bit larger as shown below:

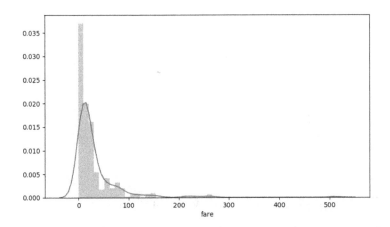

Set context

Sometimes, you may be in need of creating plots for posters. To achieve this, we can call the *set_content()* function and pass only the parameter *poster* to it as demonstrated below:

```
sns.set_context('poster')
sns.distplot(data['fare'])
```

The entire script should be as follows:

```
import numpy as np
import pandas as pd

import matplotlib.pyplot as plt
import seaborn as sns
import sys

sys.__stdout__ = sys.stdout

data = sns.load_dataset('titanic')

sns.set_context('poster')
sns.distplot(data['fare'])
plt.show()
```

The script will generate the following plot:

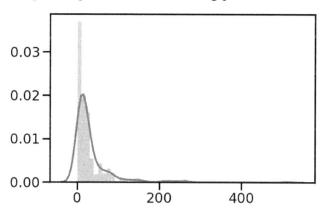

The plot shown above has poster specifications. The fonts shown on the plot are a bit larger compared to the fonts of the normal plots.

You must have seen that Seaborn is an advanced data visualization library for Python. It comes in numerous ways through which we can modify our plots.

8-Creating Maps and Visualizing Geospatial Data

Geospatial data is the type of data that has geographic components in it. The records in the dataset have locational information tied to them like geographic data in the form of coordinates, city, address, zip code, etc. The data describes the relationship between objects and space. Such data can come from satellite imagery, GPS data and geotagging.

The Dataset

In this chapter, we will be using the World Development Indicators Dataset that can be found on the Kaggle website. Here is the URL where you can find the dataset:

https://www.kaggle.com/worldbank/world-development-indicators

Just download the *Indicators.csv* dataset since it's the one we will be using. Keep it in the same folder as your Python scripts.

Since we are working with geospatial maps, the coordinates of countries are needed for plotting purposes. You will need a *world-countries.json* file that will have the coordinates of different countries. This will be provided. Download and store it in the same directory as your Python scripts.

The dataset contains more than a thousand annual indicators showing the economic development from about 247 countries located all over the world from 1960 to 2015.

Exploration

To get started, first import the required libraries. We will use the Pandas library alongside the Folium library. They can be imported as follows:

```
import folium
import pandas as pd
```

Now that the libraries have been imported, we need to set the world coordinates using the *world_countries.json* file. Here is the script for this:

```
country_geo = 'world-countries.json'
```

Let us now load the data from the *ndicators.csv* file:

```
data = pd.read_csv('Indicators.csv')
print(data.shape)
```

You should now have the following code:

```
import folium
import pandas as pd

country_geo = 'world-countries.json'

data = pd.read_csv('Indicators.csv')
print(data.shape)
```

And you should get the following result:

```
(5656458, 6)
```

The above output shows that the dataset has 5656458 rows and 6 columns. It is a large database. Let us see the first 5 rows of the dataset by invoking the *head()* function:

```
data.head()
```

If the above command returns an error, modify your code to the following:

```
import folium
import pandas as pd
import sys

sys.__stdout__ = sys.stdout

country_geo = 'world-countries.json'
```

```
data = pd.read_csv('Indicators.csv')
print(data.head())
```

The code should return the following output:

```
     CountryName CountryCode   ...    Year         Value
0    Arab World         ARB    ...    1960   1.335609e+02
1    Arab World         ARB    ...    1960   8.779760e+01
2    Arab World         ARB    ...    1960   6.634579e+00
3    Arab World         ARB    ...    1960   8.102333e+01
4    Arab World         ARB    ...    1960   3.000000e+06

[5 rows x 6 columns]
```

The dataset has different indicators for different countries, along with the year and the value for the indicator. Let us see the countries and the indicators that we have:

```
countries =
data['CountryName'].unique().tolist()
indicators =
data['IndicatorName'].unique().tolist()
print(len(countries))
print(len(indicators))
```

This will print the following:

```
247
1344
```

The output shows that we have 247 countries with 1344 levels of indicators. Let us have a look at the first 30 levels of indicators:

```
import folium
```

```
import pandas as pd
import sys

sys.__stdout__ = sys.stdout

country_geo = 'world-countries.json'

data = pd.read_csv('Indicators.csv')
countries =
data['CountryName'].unique().tolist()
indicators =
data['IndicatorName'].unique().tolist()
print(data['IndicatorName'][:30])
```

It returns the following:

```
0      Adolescent fertility rate (births per 1,000 wo...
1      Age dependency ratio (% of working-age populat...
2      Age dependency ratio, old (% of working-age po...
3      Age dependency ratio, young (% of working-age ...
4                Arms exports (SIPRI trend indicator values)
5                Arms imports (SIPRI trend indicator values)
6                     Birth rate, crude (per 1,000 people)
7                                         CO2 emissions (kt)
8                CO2 emissions (metric tons per capita)
9      CO2 emissions from gaseous fuel consumption (%...
10     CO2 emissions from liquid fuel consumption (% ...
11      CO2 emissions from liquid fuel consumption (kt)
12     CO2 emissions from solid fuel consumption (% o...
13                    Death rate, crude (per 1,000 people)
14              Fertility rate, total (births per woman)
15                      Fixed telephone subscriptions
16     Fixed telephone subscriptions (per 100 people)
17              Hospital beds (per 1,000 people)
18     International migrant stock (% of population)
19              International migrant stock, total
20         Life expectancy at birth, female (years)
21           Life expectancy at birth, male (years)
22          Life expectancy at birth, total (years)
23                   Merchandise exports (current US$)
24     Merchandise exports by the reporting economy (...
25     Merchandise exports by the reporting economy, ...
26     Merchandise exports to developing economies in...
27     Merchandise exports to developing economies in...
28     Merchandise exports to developing economies in...
29     Merchandise exports to developing economies in...
Name: IndicatorName, dtype: object
```

It seems good for us to investigate the *Life expectancy at birth, female (years)* indicator. This means that we need to pull out the data about life expectancy for all countries in the year 2013. The year has been chosen randomly:

```python
import folium
import pandas as pd
import sys


sys.__stdout__ = sys.stdout

country_geo = 'world-countries.json'

data = pd.read_csv('Indicators.csv')
countries =
data['CountryName'].unique().tolist()
indicators =
data['IndicatorName'].unique().tolist()
indicator = 'Life expectancy at birth'
year = 2013
mask1 =
data['IndicatorName'].str.contains(indicator
)
mask2 = data['Year'].isin([year])
# apply the mask
stage = data[mask1 & mask2]
print(stage.head())
```

It returns something of this sort:

```
                   CountryName CountryCode   ...    Year      Value
5377669                Arab World        ARB   ...    2013  72.536117
5377670                Arab World        ARB   ...    2013  68.848383
5377671                Arab World        ARB   ...    2013  70.631305
5378129  Caribbean small states        CSS   ...    2013  74.757382
5378130  Caribbean small states        CSS   ...    2013  69.183365

[5 rows x 6 columns]
```

We have obtained the indicators that we needed. We need to prepare our data for plotting by maintaining the country code and the values that we have plotted:

```python
import folium
import pandas as pd
import sys


sys.__stdout__ = sys.stdout

country_geo = 'world-countries.json'

data = pd.read_csv('Indicators.csv')
countries =
data['CountryName'].unique().tolist()
indicators =
data['IndicatorName'].unique().tolist()
indicator =  'Life expectancy at birth'
year = 2013
mask1 =
data['IndicatorName'].str.contains(indicator
)
mask2 = data['Year'].isin([year])
# apply the mask
stage = data[mask1 & mask2]
data_to_plot =
stage[['CountryCode','Value']]
print(data_to_plot.head())
```

The code will return the following:

	CountryCode	Value
5377669	ARB	72.536117
5377670	ARB	68.848383
5377671	ARB	70.631305
5378129	CSS	74.757382
5378130	CSS	69.183365

The name of the indicator should also be extracted since we need to use it on our plot as the legend:

```python
import folium
import pandas as pd
import sys


sys.__stdout__ = sys.stdout

country_geo = 'world-countries.json'

data = pd.read_csv('Indicators.csv')
countries =
data['CountryName'].unique().tolist()
indicators =
data['IndicatorName'].unique().tolist()
indicator =  'Life expectancy at birth'
year = 2013
mask1 =
data['IndicatorName'].str.contains(indicator
)
mask2 = data['Year'].isin([year])
# apply the mask
stage = data[mask1 & mask2]
data_to_plot =
stage[['CountryCode','Value']]
indicator = stage.iloc[0]['IndicatorName']
print(indicator)
```

It will print the following:

Life expectancy at birth, female (years)

Creating the Interactive Map

We now need to use the folium library and create an interactive map. The map will be created at a moderately high level of zoom. After that, we will use *choropleth*, which is a built-in method to attach the geographic json of the country and plot the data. Here is the code:

```python
import folium
import pandas as pd
import sys


sys.__stdout__ = sys.stdout

country_geo = 'world-countries.json'

data = pd.read_csv('Indicators.csv')
countries =
data['CountryName'].unique().tolist()
indicators =
data['IndicatorName'].unique().tolist()
indicator = 'Life expectancy at birth'
year = 2013
mask1 =
data['IndicatorName'].str.contains(indicator
)
mask2 = data['Year'].isin([year])
# apply the mask
stage = data[mask1 & mask2]
data_to_plot =
stage[['CountryCode','Value']]
indicator = stage.iloc[0]['IndicatorName']
```

```
map = folium.Map(location=[100, 0],
zoom_start=1.5)
map.choropleth(geo_data=country_geo,
data=data_to_plot,
            columns=['CountryCode',
'Value'],
            key_on='feature.id',
            fill_color='YlGnBu',
fill_opacity=0.7, line_opacity=0.2,
            legend_name=indicator)
```

The relevant parameters should also be specified. The *key on* parameter denotes the label in the json object with the country code as the feature ID attached to the border information of every country. This is the type of tie that we should create in our data. The country code in our data frame is expected to match the feature ID in our json object.

We should specify the number of aesthetics including the opacity, color scheme and labelling of the legend.

The output of the plot will be saved as an html file and it will be interactive. We need to save it then read it back to be able to interact with the map. First, we need to import the interactive html file provided by folium. Just add the following line to the top of the script:

```
from IPython.display import HTML
```

The following script can then help you to create the map and save it:

```
# Create a Folium plot
map.save('my_plot.html')
```

```
HTML('<iframe src=my_plot.html width=700
height=450></iframe>')
```

The whole script should now be as follows:

```python
import folium
import pandas as pd
import sys
from IPython.display import HTML

sys.__stdout__ = sys.stdout

country_geo = 'world-countries.json'

data = pd.read_csv('Indicators.csv')
countries =
data['CountryName'].unique().tolist()
indicators =
data['IndicatorName'].unique().tolist()
indicator =  'Life expectancy at birth'
year = 2013
mask1 =
data['IndicatorName'].str.contains(indicator
)
mask2 = data['Year'].isin([year])
# apply the mask
stage = data[mask1 & mask2]
data_to_plot =
stage[['CountryCode','Value']]
indicator = stage.iloc[0]['IndicatorName']
map = folium.Map(location=[100, 0],
zoom_start=1.5)
map.choropleth(geo_data=country_geo,
data=data_to_plot,
              columns=['CountryCode',
'Value'],
              key_on='feature.id',
              fill_color='YlGnBu',
fill_opacity=0.7, line_opacity=0.2,
```

```
                  legend_name=indicator)
# Create a Folium plot
map.save('my_plot.html')
HTML('<iframe src=my_plot.html width=700
height=450></iframe>')
```

The following map will be plotted:

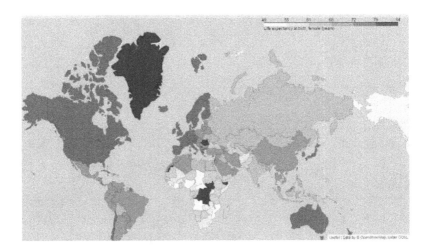

To access the map, just navigate to the directory you have saved the Python script and look for the file *my_plot.html*. Open the file on your web browser and you will get the above.

If you need to see the interactivity of the map, just create a gif file from the map.

We now have the map. Note that the darker colors shown on the map are an indication of a higher life expectancy for females.

Conclusion

This marks the end of this book. Data visualization is good and applicable everywhere. It helps individuals to identify patterns, trends, and relationships that are hard to identify in textual and numerical data. Research has shown that individuals can easily grasp concepts from graphics than from text. There are a number of graphics that can be used to represent text data. One only has to choose the best tool that they can understand with ease. The kind of graphics library to be used is also determined by the kind of data that you have. There are various tools that can be used to create a visual representation of data. Some of these tools allow the user to programmatically create graphics, while others provide their users with a graphical user interface through which they can create a visual representation of their data. You only have to choose the best tool for you.

The Python programming language is a great tool since it provides numerous tools for data visualizations. There are libraries that are good for Python beginners and those good for use by Python experts. A tool such as the Seaborn library allows its users to create plots that are more advanced compared to tools such as Pandas and Matplotlib. However, most data visualization libraries for Python were developed on top of the Matplotlib library. Data visualization is the key to faster and effective data analysis by both beginners and experts.

About the Author

Samuel Burns has a Ph.D. in Machine Learning and is an Artificial Intelligence developer, researcher, and educator as well as an Open Source Software developer. He has authored many papers as well as a number of popular software packages. Specialist in Data Mining and Security, Burns is an active machine learning researcher and regularly teaches courses and maintains resources for the data scientist.

 Burn's research has pioneered developments in ensemble learning, outlier detection and profile discovery. He is involved in numerous international artificial intelligence and data mining research activities and conferences.